COMMON STOCK
LONG TERM INVESTMENTS

BY
EDGAR LAWRENCE SMITH

PRESIDENT, INVESTMENT MANAGERS COMPANY

Martino Publishing
Mansfield Centre, CT
2012

Martino Publishing
P.O. Box 373,
Mansfield Centre, CT 06250 USA

www.martinopublishing.com

ISBN 978-1-61427-332-5

© 2012 Martino Publishing

Cover design by T. Matarazzo

Printed in the United States of America On 100% Acid-Free Paper

COMMON STOCKS AS
LONG TERM INVESTMENTS

BY
EDGAR LAWRENCE SMITH

PRESIDENT, INVESTMENT MANAGERS COMPANY

New York
THE MACMILLAN COMPANY
1928

Printed in the United States of America by
THE FERRIS PRINTING COMPANY, NEW YORK

INTRODUCTION

These studies are the record of a failure—the failure of facts to sustain a preconceived theory. This preconceived theory might be stated as follows:

While a diversity of common stocks has, without doubt, proved a more profitable investment than high-grade bonds in the period from 1897 to 1923, during which dollars were depreciating, yet with the upturn in the dollar, bonds may be relied upon to show better results than common stocks, *as they did* in the period from the close of the Civil War to 1896, during which the dollar was constantly increasing in purchasing power.

Based upon a general understanding of the results which logically follow changes in the purchasing power of the dollar, such a theory should have been demonstrable, and the tests of the comparative investment value of bonds and of common stocks covering the period from 1866 to the end of the century, which are outlined in the following pages, were undertaken in its support. But they failed, because, quite unexpectedly, they demonstrated that the premise upon which the preconceived theory rested, namely, that high-grade bonds *had* proved to be better investments during the period of appreciating dollars, could not be clearly sustained by any evidence available.

The preconceived theory was, therefore, abandoned.

The facts assembled, however, seemed worthy of further investigation. If they would not prove what we had hoped to have them prove, it seemed desirable to turn them loose and to follow them to whatever end they might lead.

Fortunately they seem to have led to the isolation of certain characteristics inherent in a diversification of representative common stocks which may be of value to those investors who have given small heed to the long-term investment attributes of this class of security, and to others, who, while drawn to common stocks, have felt that their leaning in that direction should be repressed as lacking in conservatism.

Bonds, as a class, have certain recognized attributes. A diversification of common stocks has its own attributes, which differ from those of bonds. Each class of investment has its useful purpose and its proper place in any investment plan. A clearer understanding of their differing attributes may help to determine the relative proportion of each of these two classes of securities which will best serve the investment requirements and purposes of each investor.

E. L. S.

December 9, 1924.
22 William Street, New York.

ACKNOWLEDGEMENTS

While the account of these studies is brief, their pursuit has been long, and the author wishes to acknowledge the sympathetic co-operation through discussion which he has received from many sources, notably from members of the firm of Wood, Low & Company in whose offices they were carried out, and from Theodore T. Scudder and F. Haven Clark, of the firm of Scudder, Stevens & Clark, of Boston.

Their co-operation has not stopped with the completion of this volume, but has continued in the formulation of a practical plan under which certain fundamental principles of investment management disclosed by these studies may be brought, under responsible auspices, to the service of investors.

The tables were compiled largely by Mr. W. C. Beecken.

CONTENTS

COMMON STOCKS AS LONG TERM INVESTMENTS

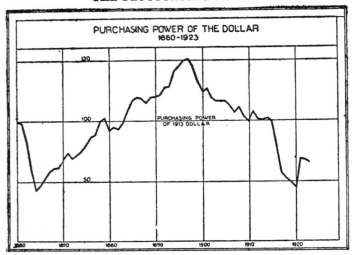

PURCHASING POWER OF THE DOLLAR
1860-1923

PURCHASING POWER
OF 1913 DOLLAR

CHART No. 1.—This chart is derived from U. S. Department of Labor
index numbers of Wholesale Commodity Prices, using their old
series, corrected, from 1860 to 1900 and the new series from 1900
on. The transfer from old to new series was made in 1900 because the transition in that year showed the smallest variation.
See U. S. Dept. of Labor Bulletin No. 149, and Monthly Labor
Review, Vol. XV, No. 1, July, 1922.

Variations in the dollar, as a measure of real value,
have an important bearing upon the advantageous investment of individual resources. A series of studies
is here presented, based on a comparison of high grade
bonds and of common stocks over different periods ex-
tending from the close of the Civil War up to 1922.
The cumulative evidence of these studies favors diversified common stocks, even in periods of appreciating
currency, such as from 1866 to 1897. Since 1897, with
currency depreciating, the diversified common stocks
selected are shown to have been by far the superior
form of long term investment.

2

COMMON STOCKS AS LONG TERM INVESTMENTS

CHAPTER I

BONDS AND THE DOLLAR

WHEN the topic of conservative investment is under discussion, high grade bonds hold an unassailable position in the minds of most people, and the discussion usually resolves itself into weighing the relative merits of different issues of such bonds or how far it is safe to stray away from the most highly secured bonds in an effort to obtain a higher income return. Those who venture to suggest preferred stocks sometimes feel that they have gone as far as conservative opinion will support them. Common stocks are ordinarily left out of the discussion altogether.

Common Stocks are, in general, regarded as a medium for Speculation—not for Long Term Investment.

Bonds, on the other hand, are generally held to be the best medium for Long Term Investment—free from the hazards of Speculation.

Is this view sound? What are the facts?

A venerable tradition of conservatism has attached to first mortgages whether upon real estate or upon corporate property as the basis for an issue of bonds. This tradition was supported by experience up to 1897, when the purchasing power of the dollar reached its highest point. But the experience of investors in real estate mortgages and in mortgage bonds, with respect to a depreciating currency since 1897 and with respect to a rising interest rate since 1902, raises grave doubt as to the justification of this tradition with particular reference to personal as opposed to institutional investments.

Because common stocks are regarded as speculative, they are frequently omitted entirely from the lists of a great many investors. Is this omission based on a thorough study of the relative merits of bonds and stocks or is it based in part on prejudice? It is true that stocks fluctuate in price in response to many factors, some related to the industry they represent, some to general business conditions, some to the temporary market position of avowed speculators.

Is it not possible that the association of speculation with common stocks has somewhat influenced a majority of investors against them, and has exaggerated in their minds the danger of possible loss to those who buy them for long term investment?

Is it not possible that the definite weakness of otherwise perfectly safe bonds is overlooked—namely, that they cannot in any way participate in the growth and increasing activity of the country—that they are defenceless against a depreciating currency?

The fundamental difference between stocks and bonds is that—

Stocks represent ownership of property and processes; their value and income return fluctuating with the earning power of the property.

Bonds represent a promise to pay a certain number of dollars at a future date with a fixed rate of interest each year during the life of the loan.

The value of stocks, expressed in dollars, increases with the growth and prosperity of the country and of the industry represented. It also increases in proportion as dollars themselves decrease in purchasing power as expressed in a higher cost of living. Stocks are subject to temporary hazards of hard times, and may be destroyed in value by a radical change in the arts or by poor management.

The value of high grade bonds, expressed in dollars, changes far less because their value represents dollars and nothing but dollars.

The only commodity whose price in terms of dollars does not vary at all (except under most extraordinary conditions) is gold. That is because a dollar is, by definition, a certain weight of gold of a certain fineness. The price is legally fixed. The price at which bonds sell participates with gold in this legal, but to a certain degree fictitious, stabilization.

Such fluctuations as do occur in the dollar price of bonds result from—

1. Changes in the credit position of the issuing company —the prospects of its being able to pay interest and principal when due. This is largely influenced by its earning power in excess of current interest requirements.

2. Changes in the current demand and supply of liquid capital, in relation to the length of the unexpired term and the fixed interest rate of the bonds in question.*

* The most reliable index of the current demand for liquid capital is found in variations in the rate commanded by commercial paper.

As the question of including well selected common stocks in a long term investment fund, as against confining such a fund to bonds alone, is to some extent related to the nature of the dollar, some space will be devoted to a discussion of the dollar as a measure of real value. If we seem to treat it with a certain amount of disrespect, it is only to emphasize its weakness. The dollar stands to-day as the soundest currency unit in the world, for which those who have shared in defending it against the assaults of free silver and have fortified it through the creation of the Federal Reserve Banking System deserve our gratitude. Nevertheless, it shares, with all currencies yet devised, certain definite weaknesses. It is vulnerable to unwise governmental action, and those governmental authorities whose duty it is to maintain its value are ever on the defensive. Labor seeking higher wages is, in part, attacking the value of the dollar; farmers seeking higher prices for their products and eager to pay off the mortgage on the farm are, in part, assailing the value of the dollar; tariff protected industries join in reducing the purchasing power of the dollar. All debtors favor a depreciating dollar. An increasing value to the dollar is accompanied by distress on the part of large portions of the community, a lessening of its value is accompanied by an appearance of great prosperity and a general feeling of well being. As a result, there is a constant struggle between those who would maintain the full purchasing power of the dollar and those whose interests lie in the other direction. As the latter are in the majority, and as they become increasingly well organized, there is no certainty that the dollar will recover the ground it has steadily lost since 1897, or that it will not again suffer such radical depreciation as occurred between 1915 and 1920.

In addition to its tendency to lose ground from the point of view of the actual commodities or services it will buy, we find the income dollar losing the power to maintain its recipient in the same relative social position due to the increasing number of commodities required to satisfy the same social standards.

The ordinary commodity index of the purchasing power of the dollar does not include this factor, which is represented, let us say, by better heating, lighting and plumbing, by automobiles instead of buggies, by telephones, radio and so on down the list of the things we have to-day that were unknown to our fathers, offset in part, only, by lower manufacturing costs due to improved machinery and quantity production. All these things call for more dollars of income. At the same time they add a corresponding value to those industries which supply them. In other words they all contribute to a more rapid circulation of money which is reflected in the dollar value of common stocks representing industries that participate in this circulation.

Among the current factors which tend to retard the recovery of value by the dollar are state and municipal expenditures. The following editorial from the New York *World* of October 8, 1923, illuminates this point:

The Budget in its current issue publishes an analysis of Federal census returns from fourteen typical States of the Union showing the costs of their Governments in 1922. These costs are exclusive of the costs of county, city and town Governments and amount to $438,690,000, or $13.21 per capita. Applied to the whole population of the United States, the figures indicate a State Government cost of $1,443,161,272 for 1922, which is more than double the cost for as recent a year as 1919 and four times the cost for 1913.

Building State roads is found to figure largely in this startling expansion of State expenditure. It is the newest thing in State activity and comparable with the railroad-building furor of seventy years ago. States are bonding themselves right and left for these improved highways and the interest cost is yet to figure in the fast-mounting construction and maintenance costs of the taxpayers. Cities, towns and counties are chipping in additional sums. The Federal Government is there as well with an actual and prospective expenditure fairly staggering. It is the day of the automobile, whose private extravagances are forcing a public extravagance in due proportion.

States as sovereign bodies have been noticeable in recent years chiefly for their shrinking place in the American scheme of government. But as free and independent debt-contractors and road-builders and tax-burdeners they are glowing with a new life.

THE DOLLAR

If it were conceivable that the length of a yard stick were influenced by changing conditions, growing longer during certain periods and shorter during other periods; if at the same time all other measures used to reduce the dimension of length to numerals adapted to computation were equally changeable; if, let us say, the meter fluctuated; if, let us further suppose, the influences which worked upon the current length of the yard stick differed from those which worked upon the current length of the meter so that the yard might be gaining in length while the meter was becoming shorter; if all these things were true, and there were no fixed standard of measurement or word to describe length that meant the same thing in one year as it did in another, it would certainly prove a great embarrassment to the engineering profession, to say nothing of the rest of us. It is hard for us to conceive how any business could be transacted, how any buildings could be erected, how any clothes could be made, and yet undoubtedly they would be.

OTHER MEASURES ARE FIXED

Fortunately this is not the case. The measure of length is a fixed thing, and from this fact, the measurement of cubical content becomes a fixed thing, derived mathematically from the measure of the length of three dimensions. The establishment of weights as fixed units becomes possible through the fact that cubic contents may be accurately measured in materials which do not vary in specific gravity. Thus even weight units are fixed only because they can be derived mathematically from the fixed unit of measure—length.

Measures of value, on the contrary, are not fixed. The Dollar to-day is a different measure from the Dollar of yesterday. The Mark of to-day—well, let us say of an hour ago—is a different measure of value from the Mark of the moment. And so it is with the Pound Sterling, the Franc, the Ruble, the Yen, and to add to the confusion, the only simple way we can describe the varying value of one fluctuating measure of value is in terms of other fluctuating measures of value.

Logically this cannot be done. But it is done. It is done solely because something has to be done, and no more satisfactory method has been devised for defining value. The best that can be said is that some measures of value are more stable than others. During one period of years it may be the Pound Sterling with which all other measures are compared; during another it may be the Dollar. But over any considerable period of time, it can be safely stated, the actual measure of true wealth or true value will change. It has never remained the same and the chances are that unless some entirely new method is found for measuring value, it never will remain the same.

IMPORTANT TO INVESTORS

This fact is of greater moment to individual investors, whose investments are made with the happiness and comfort of their children in mind, than is usually supposed. "Safety of principal," yes—that is the first essential. But what is "principal"—is it merely the obligation of some sound organization to repay a certain number of fluctuating measures of value at a future date? What if, at the date of repayment, the measure has shrunk to one-half of its present size? Has the principal been safeguarded? To show that this is not a thought that should be dismissed as pure theory, it seems worth while to refer to an editorial which appeared in the New York *World*, July 12, 1923, apropos "Dollar Wheat."

Time was when "dollar wheat" was the familiar slogan and maximum demand of the American farmer. But that was when the dollar would buy something over and above the cost of producing a bushel of wheat. Now the dollar will buy little more than half as much, and for a bushel of wheat falls short of the cost of production.

There is no doubt that the wheat farmer's dollar had shrunk. If it had been a yard stick in the days when dollar wheat sounded like a high price, it would have been only a trifle over 18 inches long at the time this editorial appeared.

If it is true, then, that the dollar may shrink in value, and that an investment in bonds is defenceless against such shrinkage, how does it come about that the most conservative of our great financial institutions invest so great a proportion of their total assets in bonds re-payable in dollars?

There is a vast difference between the investment needs and purposes of such institutions from those of the individual investor, or the family estate. Take an insurance company for example. It is by the nature of its business perfectly safeguarded against any possible loss through the depreciation of the dollar. It deals in nothing but dollars. Its contracts call for the payment of future dollars. It therefore requires to know only that it will receive from its investments more future dollars than it will have to pay out. The purchasing power of those future dollars is of no concern to it. If dollars have shrunk in value, the beneficiary under its policies absorbs the shrinkage, the company does not.

BANKS AND INSURANCE COMPANIES

The same is true of savings banks, commercial banks and trust companies. Their investments are all made to protect dollar obligations. Their sole concern is so to conduct their affairs that they will always have available more dollars than they will be called upon, under their commitments, to pay out, at the same time deriving a profit above operating expenses. It is natural and right that the highly trained specialists whom they employ to guide them in their financial policies, should concentrate their attention upon promissory obligations payable in a fixed number of dollars, amply safeguarded against the shrinkage in value of the particular properties by which they are secured, even though they are not in the least safeguarded against the possible shrinkage in the purchasing power of the dollar itself. These financial institutions are also subject to the necessity, at times, of converting a very substantial part of their investments into liquid or currency form, which is not normally true of the individual investor who has the future welfare of his family as his main investment purpose.

These institutions are called upon periodically to present a balance sheet of assets and liabilities in the form of annual statements, etc., and cannot afford to take the chance of having their security holdings show temporary shrinkage in *market* * value at the time such reports are published. To an individual a temporary decline in the market quotations on his security

---

* Many financial institutions are protected by law or by the rulings of the governmental departments under which they operate against the necessity of reporting the current market value of their maturing obligations. They report only the amortized value of such securities, on the theory that they will hold them to maturity and be paid in full. This situation results from necessity, as the fall in the market value of bonds between 1901 and 1920 would otherwise have placed some such institutions in an embarrassing position. There is no basis upon which the value of stocks may be figured with any degree of safety, other than their current market price.

holdings is not of such serious import, provided he knows that his assets are sound and of real value. Furthermore, he is subject to no laws as to what he may or may not invest in, and for this reason, if for no other, he should at least study the possibilities of profitable investment in securities which the larger institutional investors are prevented by law from considering, and which for that reason may be selling upon a basis of higher income return.

Is it not possible that individual investors are unduly influenced by the well deserved reputations of such financial institutions for conservative investment, and overlook the fact that they, as individuals, are investing with the purpose of providing real wealth, not the changing symbol of value for their later years, or for the next generation?

CHAPTER II

BONDS AND COMMON STOCKS

There are, of course, a wide variety of bonds. But as this discussion is confined to the question of conservative long term investment, we need consider only those bonds which, at the time of purchase, are regarded as well secured by mortgage or prior lien on property which has been authoritatively appraised as worth well in excess of the total amount of bonds issued against it. It is worth while to call attention to the fact that such appraisals are largely based on the cost of construction, or the cost of reproducing the properties, and that such costs alone are no criterion of the real value of the properties at a later date, if a change occurs in the industry that renders a part or all of the property obsolete, or if the construction or location of the property was not wisely planned in connection with the business to be done.

NATURE OF SECURITY

A bond secured by a mortgage on a stretch of railway, and representing only 50% of the cost of the railway under mortgage, will not be a safe investment if the traffic over this particular stretch of trackage yields a net income insufficient to pay the interest charges on the bonds. In a reorganization this stretch

14

of road may be abandoned to its bondholders, who will find themselves in the railroad business upon most unpromising terms.

Likewise the invention of new and more economical machinery may render the plant of a manufacturing company practically worthless without regard to its original cost or the cost of reproducing it.

Therefore, it is of the greatest importance, in the selection of bonds for long term investment, to get all the assurance possible that the revenues, after operating expenses of the debtor company, are and will continue to be, during the whole period that the bonds are to be held, well in excess of all fixed charges, and will provide ample funds for depreciation and possible obsolescence; that the margin over all fixed charges will be ample to afford the company the best of credit so that changes in plant or extensions may be financed in part at least through the sale of stock on favorable terms. A company whose net earnings are so meager that it can finance necessary expansion or changes only through the creation of new debt, may, in the end, prove unsatisfactory to even its underlying mortgage bondholders, and if any danger of this can be foreseen at the time the purchase of its bonds is under consideration, they cannot, except in unusual instances, be regarded as investments of the most conservative character. In other words, the highest degree of conservatism in the purchase of bonds for long term investment implies the selection of bonds issued by companies whose operations promise over a long term of years to yield profits well in excess of all possible demands of its funded debt and other overhead charges.

Such profits will, in the course of events, accrue to the holders of the common stock of these companies.

SAFE BONDS IMPLY SAFE STOCKS

If, then, the judgment which has dictated the selection of bonds has been sound, the holder of the bonds will receive his interest payments with complete regularity and the holders of the common stock of the same companies will receive dividends, not with the same regularity, perhaps, but with the offsetting chance that he will receive something more than a normal return on his investment through increased earnings and distribution.   Theoretically, if the dollar *depreciates* in value during the period of investment, his stock will rise in dollar value to a corresponding degree, and his income will increase correspondingly, and, theoretically, if the dollar *appreciates* in value during the same period, he will lose on a corresponding scale.   Conversely—while the income from the bond will be constant, its real value to the investor who holds it will fluctuate with the dollar, decreasing as the dollar decreases in value and increasing as the dollar increases. And similarly the principal of a bond, representing nothing but dollars, will increase and decrease in real value with the dollar.

WHERE DOES THIS REASONING LEAD US?

Let us assume, for the moment, that this reasoning has made it seem worth while to give serious consideration to the common stocks of companies whose bonds are regarded as highly attractive on account of the wide margin of earnings in excess of fixed charges that their operations seem to promise over the long term. We then cannot escape the thought that if these same companies had no bonded debt at all, their common stocks would present features of still greater interest. This opens the way to the consideration of common stocks as a class, without reference to whether they are preceded by bonds or not.

Having allowed our minds to stray thus far from the paths of orthodox doctrine as applied to the most conservative investment policies, we should refuse to consider any further theorizing on the relative merits of stocks and bonds for long term investment until some practical facts are brought forth to support or to disprove the thoughts that our reasoning has allowed us to harbor. Surely, after reviewing the large number of companies whose operations have proved unfavorable to stockholders, even if they have not actually resulted in total loss, no individual investor out of touch with active business would consider for a moment putting his strictly long time investment funds into anything but the most highly secured mortgage bonds, letting the "Business men" take all the risks involved in common stocks! Well—let us see how it would work out if our fathers had invested solely in common stocks, not with the thought of immediate speculative gain, a thought that it is unfortunately most difficult to eliminate from the choice of common stocks, but with the sober-minded purpose of providing

1. Constancy of Income.
2. Safety of Principal.

Constancy or regularity of income is placed first because it is the factor that is ordinarily considered to be most àt hazard in common stocks as contrasted with bonds.

CHAPTER III

In the tests that follow, the only principle of sound investment that has been applied to the selection of stocks is that of diversification. Without diversification, the purchase of common stocks cannot be considered.

It was necessary to eliminate any real judgment in the selection of particular stocks because of the danger of unconsciously basing this judgment upon facts which have become known subsequent to the supposed date of purchase.

METHOD OF SELECTION

In each test an arbitrary method of selecting the stocks has been set up before the selection is made. The stocks are then taken according to this arbitrary method, thus eliminating every possibility that the knowledge of subsequent events has colored our choice. In fact, in one case at least, a stock which might well have fallen into the group chosen was eliminated because there was an element of doubt as to whether or not it would have come strictly within the formula established, and knowledge of the extraordinarily favorable experience that stockholders in this company have had, made it unavailable for the test.

18

RESEARCH

The history of each stock selected as it appears in published records has been studied and tabulated. The working tables are too large to be included in this volume. They have been carefully checked, however, and the totals given herein are believed to be correct arithmetically. It is recognized that a few errors may have crept into the original tables because of uncertainties as to the exact meaning of some of the recorded data. When the doubt seemed likely to materially affect the result of the test, the stock has been sold out at current quotations. We have in no case changed our original list of stocks in a test, because of difficulty in determining the history of any stock. Occasionally we have been unable to find quotations for "rights," and have, therefore, failed to give full credit to income account.

The aim has been to favor stocks in no way, while every effort has been made to give all possible advantage to bonds in the comparison.

IMPORTANCE OF TESTS

The importance of these tests lies in their cumulative force. No single test would have more than passing significance. But all of them together are strongly indicative of underlying factors which have been overlooked by too large a proportion of individual investors.

Each test assumes the investment of approximately $10,000 in ten diversified common stocks of large companies and an investment of an equal amount in high grade bonds. They cover the entire period from 1866 to date, and the supposed purchase of stocks is made without reference to the condition of the stock market at the time of purchase except in those tests where a peak in the market has been deliberately chosen (Tests 7 and 8).

Every test except one shows better results are obtained from common stocks than from bonds, as follows:

Period	Total Advantage of Stocks over Bonds
Test No. 1, 1901-1922 (22 years)	$16,400.94
Test No. 2, 1901-1922 (22 years)	9,242.26
Test No. 3, 1901-1922 (22 years)	21,954.72
Test No. 4, 1880-1899 (20 years)	12,002.04
Test No. 5, 1866-1885 (20 years)	2,966.85
Test No. 6, 1866-1885 (20 years)	- 1,012.00
Test No. 7, 1892-1911 (20 years)	11,723.80
Test No. 8, 1906-1922 (17 years)	6,651.01
Test No. 8a, 1906-1922 (17 years)	4,938.08
Test No. 9, 1901-1922 (22 years), Railroads	13,734.72
Test No. 10, 1901-1922 (22 years), Railroads	3,329.72
Test No. 11, 1901-1922 (22 years), Railroads	17,140.25

The methods by which the stocks were selected are not recommended to an investor actually investing to-day, but they are important in judging the results of the tests. Sound investment counsel at the time purchases are made, and applied constantly to the holdings would, without any doubt, have greatly improved the showing made.

Test No. 1—1901-1922

The period selected for this test was dictated by the circumstance that the first volume of the Commercial and Financial Chronicle that was readily available was for the year 1901. A glance at the Dow, Jones chart showing average prices of stocks indicated that January, 1901, was not a particularly low area. In fact, based on earlier prices, it must have been regarded at the time as a fairly high market, not quite so high as the average for 1899, but very much higher than 1897, 1898 or 1900.* If anything, our supposed investor would have hesitated to invest, for long term holding, at so high an indicated price range, following as it did, the rapid rise in securities during the last few months of 1900. However, we forced him to buy in the first full week in January, 1901, namely, the week ending January 12th of that year.

Not wishing to give him the advantage of any knowledge that we might now have of events following 1901, we forced him to a hit-or-miss policy which could only be regarded as reckless.

We assumed that he had only $10,000 and we made him pick out the ten industrial common stocks in which there had been the largest number of transactions during the week selected. This is not what a thoughtful investor would do—but it completely eliminated any chance of his making a selection based on happenings which could not have been foretold at the time the purchase was made.

*In our later pages we point out the fallacy of relying upon a majority of the charts now published, which purport to show the movement in common stock values, through the use of average quotations.

The ten stocks selected by this method were the following:

TEST No. 1—1901-1922

No. of Shares Traded in Week Ending January 13, 1901	Common Stock	No. of Shares	Average Price Week of Jan. 13, '01	Amount Invested
288,365	American Sugar Refining....	7	$140	$980
161,475	American Tobacco	18	56	1,008
158,260	Continental Tobacco	25	40	1,000
147,970	People's Gas Lt. & Coke (Chi.)	10	104	1,040
95,810	Tenn. Coal & Iron	15	64	960
94,256	Western Union Tel.	12	83	996
80,354	Federal Steel	18	56	1,008
66,398	Amalgamated Copper	11	92	1,012
54,015	Amer. Smelting & Refining...	18	55	990
52,897	Amer. Tin Plate	18	56	1,008

Total investment $10,002

During this first week in January, 1901, 15 high grade railroad bonds were selling on a basis to yield 3.95%.* But we will assume that the fund with which our supposed investor is competing was invested during the same week on a basis to yield him an uninterrupted income of 4% annually and that his selection of bonds was perfect so that none of them lost any value due to poor credit or rising interest rates during the period from 1901 to 1923.†

In addition to regular and extra dividends on stocks held over a period of years, there are stock dividends and rights to subscribe for additional stock to be accounted for.

In order to put our supposed investor on a par with the competing bond purchaser it is necessary to assume

* Standard Daily Trade Service Bulletin No. 10, October 20, 1923.
† Regarding principal value of bonds at the end of the test see **Appendix III,** first paragraph.

that he had no other resources with which to take advantage of rights to subscribe for additional stock and therefore sold such rights at the average price obtainable during the first 30 days in which they were quoted. In like manner he was forced to sell any fractional share of stock that might come to him in a stock dividend. The proceeds of such sales were credited to current income. All whole shares of stock received in stock dividends were retained but not credited to income. They tended to increase his subsequent annual income on account of receiving dividends on the increased number of shares held, and they tended to increase the capital value of his holdings on the dates selected for checking up this factor in his investment.

These dates were December 31, 1913—just prior to any thought of the world war, and December 31, 1922.

The list of securities held at these dates differed somewhat from the original list owing to consolidations and dissolutions. The gain in capital value, however, was shown to be as follows:

Original purchase price, January, 1901.......... $10,002
Market value, December 31, 1913.............. 13,718
Market value, December 31, 1922.............. 15,422

The above increase in market value was not perhaps so surprising as the fact that he suffered no falling off in income that brought his annual cash receipts as low in any single year as the 4% basis which he would have received on his bonds.

The annual cash income from his stock holdings is shown below. As his holdings amounted to $10,000, the annual rate of return on his investment is obvious:

INCOME TEST No. 1

Year	Cash Income	Year	Cash Income
1901	$818.10	1912	$1,039.81
1902	589.50	1913	1,051.50
1903	563.50	1914	879.25
1904	510.00	1915	735.97
1905	702.50	1916	1,047.00
1906	1,041.00	1917	1,410.75
1907	876.21	1918	1,408.50
1908	857.85	1919	925.50
1909	908.25	1920	961.50
1910	1,068.50	1921	774.75
1911	868.00	1922	743.00

Total income from stocks (22 yrs.)......... $19,780.94
Income on bonds at 4% (22 yrs.)............ 8,800.00

Excess income from stocks over bonds....... $10,980.94

It will be noted that the year of lowest income return from stocks was 1904 when he received 5.1% on his investment against 4% on his bonds.

Total advantage of stocks over bonds is here shown:

* Increase in market price of stocks, 1901-1922.....$5,420.00
Excess income from stocks over bonds............10,980.94

Total advantage of stocks over bonds...........$16,400.94

It is recognized that the period selected for this first test was obviously (in retrospect) one that particularly favored industrial stocks, being one in which the dollar is known to have depreciated in value, as well as one in which the expansion of industrial activity was very great. Later tests cover other periods, but before passing it is worth noting that the regularity of income in this first test was maintained through two severe industrial depressions, and the greatest war in history.

* Regarding principal value of bonds at the end of the test see Appendix III, first paragraph.

Test No. 2—1901-1922

It was felt that while the haphazard choice of stocks selected in Test No. 1, which were taken merely on the basis of current popular interest in one week, had resulted in favor of common stocks over bonds as far as regularity and amount of income was concerned as well as with regard to ultimate increase in principal value, it was not fair to assume that a careful investor would pick his stocks on such a thoughtless basis.

Test No. 2, therefore, while covering the same period, is based on securities selected with somewhat more prudence. Again every precaution is taken against introducing any possibility of the choice being influenced by present knowledge of events.

On pages 1348 to 1351 of Poor's Manual for the year 1901 appears a list of Miscellaneous Industrial stocks with their dividend records from 1894 to 1900. From this list were taken those stocks which showed the most consistent dividend record for that period, some 19 companies. These were then listed and the prices at which they could have been bought during the week ending January 12, 1901, were set opposite each. The dividends paid in 1900 were then taken as a basis for determining the yield obtainable on the purchase price, and the ten stocks showing the highest yield were assumed to have been bought to the amount nearest to $1,000 worth of each stock.

Some of these stocks were not purchasable on the New York Stock Exchange, but all were quoted in the Commercial and Financial Chronicle January 12, 1901.

The list so derived was as follows:

TEST No. 2—1901-1922

Common Stock	Div. Paid 1900	Quoted Week of 1/12/01	Yield on Price	No. Shares Bought	Amount Invested
1 Diamond Match Co..........	10%	$131	7.63%	8	$1,048
2 Swift & Co.	7	102	6.85	10	1,020
3 Erie Tel. & Tel. Co.	5	75	6.67	13	975
4 Amer. Dist. Tel. Co.	2¼	34	6.6	30	1,020
5 Proctor & Gamble Co.	20	325	6.15	3	975
6 Standard Oil Co.	48	805	5.95	1	805
7 Central & So. Am. Tel. Co. ...	6	102	5.88	10	1,020
8 Amer. Sugar Ref. Co.	7.75	140	5.53	7	980
9 Westinghouse El. & Mfg. Co..	5.75	54	5.32	19	1,026
10 American Tobacco Co.	6	56	5.31	18	1,008

Total investment $9,877

In following these stocks through, we are confronted by two cases where the holder would have had to sell out, on the assumption that he had no funds with which to meet an assessment against his stock.

On this basis he sold out his Erie Tel. & Tel. in 1902 for $195 which he had purchased the year before for $975, a loss of $780 in his capital account the first year. It is reasonable to assume that with even moderately good financial counsel he would have avoided the purchase of such a stock, but in order not to be influenced in the least by facts which have become apparent since the date of purchase, this stock is left in the list.

For the same reason he would have sold his Westinghouse Electric and Mfg. Co. in 1908 for $513, for which he had paid $1,026 in 1901, a loss of $513.

In 1919, The American District Telegraph Company of New York was dissolved. Nearly all the stock was owned by the Western Union Telegraph Co. No published record of what a minority stockholder received could be found and the latter company failed to furnish us with any enlightening information, so we have assumed that this stock was sold in January, 1919, at the quoted price of 17, bringing $510 against the original investment of $1,020, or a loss of $510.

For the purpose of completing the test on a basis which seemed reasonable, yet not favoring our contention regarding the safety of common stocks, we have assumed in the income account that the proceeds of these sales were invested on a basis to yield 4% and that the cash received remained unchanged at December 31, 1913, and December 31, 1922, when the value of his capital holdings are checked, as follows:

Original purchase price, January, 1901........$9,877.00
Market value, December 31, 1913.............. 9,229.50
Market value, December 31, 1922..............10,830.00

INCOME TEST No. 2, 1901-1922

Year	Cash Income	Year	Cash Income
1901	$607.25	1912	$665.42
1902	741.88	1913	827.51
1903	678.87	1914	657.24
1904	732.80	1915	657.74
1905	752.80	1916	1,097.57
1906	1,072.05	1917	963.51
1907	798.80	1918	849.26
1908	727.80	1919	737.66
1909	864.50	1920	816.66
1910	763.30	1921	712.91
1911	690.30	1922	673.43

Total income from stocks (22 yrs.)......$17,089.26
Income at 4% on bonds (22 yrs.)*...... 8,800.00

Excess income from stocks over bonds.. $8,289.26

It is interesting to note that this list, chosen with more regard to the past record of the companies involved, than to the popularity of the securities on the

* See Test No. 1.

market at the time of purchase, did not result as favorably, either in total income return or in enhancement of capital value, yet it showed a decidedly more favorable result than the most conservative bonds yielding 4%.

The total advantage of stocks over bonds in this test is shown below:

Increase in market price of stocks, 1901-1922.. $953.00
Excess income from stocks over bonds 8,289.26

Total advantage of stocks over bonds $9,242.26

Before leaving this period we will make one more test based upon a more sensible diversification of holdings, namely, diversification by industries. This has been left to the last because in making a selection of stocks on any basis other than purely mechanical, there is the danger of being influenced by knowledge of events subsequent to the date of purchase. Let it be said, however, that this selection is made in the spirit of research and as fairly as possible representing the point of view of an investor with no great knowledge of industrial conditions but persuaded to pick one company—if possible the most representative—in each of ten different industries.

TEST No. 3—1901-1922

In attempting to put ourselves in the mental position of an investor in 1901 who has decided to invest $10,000 in ten different industries, aiming to select the most promising common stock in each industry yet possessing no special facilities for getting any but the most superficial information regarding the various stocks available, we have again turned to the Commercial and Financial Chronicle of January 12, 1901.

Here we find a complete list of Stock Exchange securities quoted by months in the year 1900. From this we take only those which were quoted in every month of 1900, thus eliminating all which were traded in only spasmodically during that year, and also those stocks which came into existence (on the Exchange) in 1900.

We find them grouped under the headings "Express Co's."—"Coal and Mining"—"Various."

We, therefore, determine to take one "Express Co.," one "Coal and Mining Co.," and one each out of the various industries into which "Various" can be logically divided.

To determine which we shall buy, under each group, we decide to buy the one that has the largest number of transactions in each group during the week of January 12, 1901—thus following the crowd.

It is important to repeat that these methods of selecting stocks are strictly laboratory methods, enabling us to eliminate present-day judgment from our tests. They are not to be followed in actually making an investment, when the highest degree of informed judgment should be applied to the selection.

On this basis we, however, have the following:

TEST No. 3, 1901-1922

No. of Shares Traded in wk. of Jan. 12, 1901	Common Stock	Price	No. Shs.	Amount Invested
1,098	U. S. Express Co.	57	18	$1,026
95,810	Tenn. Coal & Iron	64	15	960
9,356	Am. Car & Foundry	22	45	990
80,354	Federal Steel	56	18	1,008
288,365	Am. Sugar Ref.	140	7	980
94,256	Western Union Tel.	83	12	996
192,270	Brooklyn Rapid Tran.	83	12	996
147,970	People's Gas Lt. & Coke (Chicago)	104	10	1,040
161,475	American Tobacco	56	18	1,008
30,535	U. S. Rubber	28	36	1,008

Total investment $10,012

The increase in capital value of securities held would have been as follows:

Original purchase price, January, 1901........$10,012.00
Market value, December 31, 1913............. 15,335.50
Market value, December 31, 1922............. 20,602.00

INCOME TEST No. 3—1901-1922

Year	Cash Income	Year	Cash Income
1901	$616.60	1912	$985.15
1902	515.00	1913	1,049.00
1903	595.50	1914	1,008.75
1904	394.00	1915	805.00
1905	481.00	1916	809.00
1906	732.00	1917	1,230.25
1907	673.21	1918	1,168.50
1908	763.85	1919	1,663.04
1909	824.75	1920	1,640.54
1910	962.75	1921	1,319.79
1911	813.00	1922	1,114.04

Total income from stocks (22 yrs.)......$20,164.72
Income at 4% on bonds (22 yrs.)*........ 8,800.00

Excess income from stocks over bonds....$11,364.72

*See Test No. 1.

The total advantage of stocks over bonds for the period would have been as follows:

Increase in market price of stocks, 1901-1922...$10,590.00
Excess income from stocks over bonds 11,364.72

Total advantage of stocks over bonds $21,954.72

In 1904 the income from stocks held, falls $6.00 below the 4% assigned to bonds, otherwise it remains well above the return from bonds in each year.

Attention is called to the decidedly more favorable results obtained from well diversified stocks chosen on the strictly mechanical bases of Tests Nos. 1 and 3 as compared with Test No. 2. Like knowledge, a little analysis is a dangerous thing.

It is, nevertheless, to be supposed that thorough technical analysis in the selection of stocks would show possibilities of even greater returns with the safety of diversification maintained. And yet there is a definite hazard connected with digging too deep for technical reasons justifying higher yield. A broad, general view has its distinct advantages.

The Fluctuating Dollar Applied to Test No. 3—1901-1922

Enough has been said concerning the varying values represented by the fluctuating purchasing power of the dollar to show that our studies with regard to safety of principal, and our views of the real merits of an investment, are not in proper perspective if we leave this element out of the picture. The figures shown in the tests give a correct idea of the relative position of the capital value of our selection of stocks and of bonds at the end of our test, but they leave a false impression that it seems well to try to correct. The impression is that the stocks purchased at $10,000 in 1901 and sold at $20,602 in 1922 have experienced a great *speculative* gain, while bonds purchased at $10,000 and worth $10,000 at the end of the test have remained stable. Whereas, in fact, stocks have experienced only a slight gain in real value while bonds have experienced a marked *speculative* decline measured by the purchasing power of the dollar.

An attempt is made to show this in Chart No. 2.

This chart is not as easily read as are most charts because the vertical scale represents two distinct measures of value. With regard to all data shown on the chart (with one exception), this vertical scale represents purchasing power in dollars of 1901. The line AX represents 10,000 of such dollars.

The one exception referred to is the vertical solid block (❙) showing high and low quotations in each year on the total holding of our supposed investor in stocks. These blocks have been drafted on the uncorrected dollar basis. With regard to them every point on the line AX represents 10,000 dollars of the year in which they are quoted.

The fluctuating double line (=) A B, represents variations in the purchasing power of $10,000 from year to year.

Taking this line (A B) as $10,000 in each year we apply the same high and low quotations on the new scale thus created * and in the vertical hollow blocks

---

* This is done by the use of the Smith-Beeken chart, which greatly facilitates such corrections.

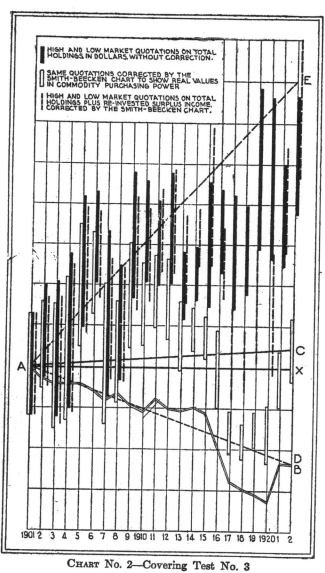

CHART No. 2—Covering Test No. 3

([]) we have represented the course of the value of our holdings in real purchasing value. The horizontal lines of the scale then show us the movement of these values with respect to the dollar of 1901 (the dollar that we invested).

Point C then represents $20,602, the value of our *stock holdings* at the end of the test, in terms of the dollar of 1901.

Point D then represents $10,000, the value of our *bonds* at the end of the test, in terms of the dollar of 1901.

Line A C shows the slight increase in real value of our stock holdings, while line A D shows the marked loss in real value of our bond holdings.

It is interesting to note in passing that the high market quotations on this group of stocks in dollars (1919 and 1920), coincided with their lowest value as measured by purchasing power ([]).

The vertical broken lines (¦) represent the high and low quotations on our original stock holdings plus an annual reinvestment of surplus income from stocks over the income received from bonds, on a corrected dollar basis.   This is fully described under Supplementary Test No. 3, page 106.

CHAPTER IV

COMPARISON BETWEEN COMMON STOCKS AND BONDS, 1866-1899

So far, our tests have been confined to twenty-two years of the present century, and while it is probably true that in respect of organization, management policies and numerous other factors, this period will be found more nearly comparable to the twenty years that lie before us than the period from 1866 to 1900, yet in one important respect it differs from the earlier period, namely, from 1897 to date we have experienced a depreciating dollar. The depreciation from 1897 to 1913 was gradual. Upon declaration of war in 1914 the depreciation became rapid until it reached its climax in May, 1920. Appreciation has followed for a time rapidly, but now we are in a period where opinions differ as to the future course of the value of the dollar. If it follows the course indicated in the periods following both the Napoleonic Wars and our own Civil War, the dollar may be expected gradually to appreciate in value for a period of from 25 to 40 years. But there are too many factors bearing on the situation to-day that are different from those which were apparent in the earlier periods, for us to be able to prophesy with certainty as to the future course of dollar values beyond saying with some degree of assurance that they will continue to fluctuate.

APPRECIATING DOLLARS

It is important, then, for us to make some test of our theory regarding common stocks as safe long term investments, covering a period when the dollar is known to have been appreciating in value as measured by its purchasing power in staple commodities.   Such a period can be found between 1864 and 1897.   As we go backward in the years, however, we find that investment conditions are ever more divergent from those which are in force to-day.   We, therefore, first take the period from 1880 to 1900 as combining a period of appreciating currency with industrial and investment conditions as nearly parallel to our own as possible.

In 1880, Industrial Stocks had no such prominence in the investment world as they have to-day.   Railroad shares held the center of the stage.   In the quotation records of the day no figures are given of the number of shares traded in, except for railroad shares.   The resulting list is the least diversified of our tests, due to the meager choice to be found in the "Miscellaneous" group on the New York Stock Exchange in 1880, a contrast with to-day's list that is not without meaning to the investor of to-day.

Thus he was to buy 5 railroad and 5 miscellaneous stocks, each to the extent of $1,000, making his total investment approximately $10,000 as in the other tests.

To do this we took the fifteen rails that had the largest number of transactions during the first week of 1880 and from these selected the five that showed the highest dividend yield on a purchase price based on the average quotation for the week.

The "Miscellaneous" were chosen without regard to

transactions because these were not recorded, and represent the five stocks quoted that week which showed the highest dividend yield on the purchase price; an unfavorable basis, as we have shown in Test No. 2.

The list so derived comprised the following stocks:

TEST No. 4—1880-1899

Stock	Div. Rate 1879	Pur. Price Jan., 1880	Yield on Pur. Price	No. Shs.	Amount Invested
Adams Express Co.	8%	106	7.55%	10	$1,060
American Express Co.	4	58	6.9	17	986
Wells Fargo Exp. Co.	8	105	7.56	10	1,050
Lake Shore & Mich. So. Ry.....	8	100	8.	10	1,000
Chi. & N. W. R. R.............	7	91	6.6	11	1,001
Mich. Central R. R.	8	90	8.8	11	990
Del., Lack. & Western	2.50	42	5.95	24	1,008
Pullman Palace Car	8	105	7.56	10	1,050
Chi., Mil. & St. Paul	5	76	6.6	13	988
Western Union Tel.	7.	103	6.8*	10	1,030

Total investment $10,163

As previously stated this test covers a period of years during which the purchasing power of the dollar in commodities was increasing. If no other factor was at work we would expect to find that the capital values of our holdings in common stock had decreased, as expressed in terms of dollars—certainly up to 1897 when the value of the dollar was at the highest point it reached between the Civil War and the present date. But some other factor is at work and contrary to expectation we find our holdings to have increased in dollar value as follows:

Original purchase price, January, 1880 ....$10,163
Market value, December 31, 1896................ 13,616
Market value, December 31, 1899................ 18,817

* Plus extra dividends.

Using the same basis for figuring income that we used in our previous tests, namely, that all rights and fractional shares are sold and the proceeds credited to current income, while whole shares received in stock dividends are held without credit to income, we find the annual cash returns from holding the above list of common stocks from January, 1880, to December 31, 1899:

INCOME TEST No. 4—1880-1899

Year	Cash Income	Year	Cash Income
1880*	$739.00	1890	$671.75
1881	879.62	1891	677.00
1882*	923.50	1892	734.50
1883†	843.75	1893	654.50
1884*	800.00	1894	724.50
1885	629.50	1895	650.00
1886	622.00	1896	687.00
1887†	654.00	1897	700.00
1888†	673.50	1898	885.14
1889	651.00	1899	727.78

Total income from stocks (20 yrs.)........$14,528.04
Income from bonds at 5.5% (20 yrs.)‡...... 11,180.00

Excess income from stocks over bonds...... $3,348.04

The total advantage of stocks over bonds in this test is shown as follows:

Increase in market price of stocks, 1880-1899‡..$8,654.00
Excess income from stocks over bonds......... 3,348.04

Total advantage of stocks over bonds.......$12,002.04

* In 1880, '82 and '84, the Chicago, Milwaukee & St. Paul Ry. issued rights for which no market quotations could be found.

† In 1883, '87 and '88, the Pullman Palace Car Co. issued rights for which no market quotations could be found.

In both of these cases the undoubted value of such rights has been omitted, so that our income account shows a lower return in these years than would actually have been received.

‡ Standard Daily Trade Service Bulletin No. 10, October 20, 1923. See also Appendix III for study of income and market price of a group of bonds for this period.

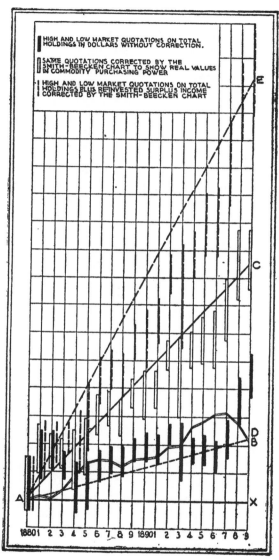

CHART No. 3—Covering Test No. 4

The Fluctuating Dollar Applied to Test No. 4—1880-1899

Chart No. 3 is constructed on the same principles as Chart No. 2, in order to show the relative movement of the real values of our stock holdings in Test No. 4 as compared with the movement in the real values of a like investment in high grade bonds.

With regard to the vertical solid blocks, the line AX represents $10,000 in each year without correction.

The line AB shows the increasing purchasing power of the dollar between 1880 and 1899 in terms of the dollar of 1880. All other data are then charted on the basis of this new scale.

Point C then represents $18,817, the value of our *stock holdings* at the end of the test, in terms of the dollar of 1880.

Point D then represents $10,000, the value of our *bonds* at the end of the test, in terms of the dollar of 1880.

The line AC shows that in spite of an appreciating dollar, our stock holdings increased in real value, to a greater extent than did bonds, represented by the line AD.

The line AE and the vertical broken lines again show the course, in real values, of our original holdings in stock plus a reinvestment of surplus income. This is fully described in Supplementary Test No. 4, page 109.

The Supplementary Tests referred to are not important to our present discussion, but are to be considered in connection with the development of a sound investment policy which is discussed in our later pages.

TEST No. 5—1866-1885

The period following our Civil War was one which, in some respects at least, resembled the present period. Prices of all commodities had been greatly inflated and the dollar (paper) in 1864 was of less value than it has been at any time since until the period from 1918 up to the crash in commodity prices in the fall of 1920, which continued in 1921.

For the purposes of our study, it seemed desirable to discover a group of common stock investments concerning which records could be found covering a term following 1866. For this purpose we turned to "Martin's Boston Stock Market—88 years," *i.e.,* 1798 to 1886. This record covers mostly New England stocks. Yet it is true that New England at that time was the center of industrial activity to a greater extent than it has been during the last 30 years, and, therefore, may be accepted as typical.

1866 SIMILAR TO 1923

1866 was chosen, rather than 1864, because by 1866 the purchasing power of the dollar had been two years on its way to recovery from the low of 1864, just as in 1921 and 1922 it recovered appreciably from its low of 1920.

In the absence of other data, we are at liberty to assume that our hypothetical investor lived in Boston in the year 1866 and was subject to the influences of the Boston financial psychology of the time.

It is beyond all question that in 1866 in Boston he would think first of cotton mill stocks—representing the great New England industry of the time. We are justified in having him buy into 3 of the largest cotton mills, namely:

Amoskeag .... Capital (1871) $3,000,000
Pacific Mills .... Capital (1871) 2,500,000
Merrimack .... Capital (1871) 2,500,000

There were no other mills rated at over $2,000,000 in 1871 (the record for 1866 not being available).

The next group in importance would seem to have been railroads. Again basing his choice on the size of the company as indicated by the amount of common stock issued, he would have chosen:

New York Central & Hudson River..... Capital (1871) $90,000,000
Reading R. R. .... Capital (1871) 27,471,300

Gas Light Companies were another important classification in the list of 1866 and on the basis of size we will assign our investor:

Boston Gas & Light Company.
Cambridge Gas Light Company.

Next came horse car lines of which he would buy on the basis of size:

Metropolitan (horse) Railway (Boston).
Cambridge (horse) Railway.

It is difficult to include what we would now term an industrial stock, other than cotton mills, of any magnitude, but we find one of some proportions for that date in Douglas Axe, which we include to give greater diversification to his list.

The prices quoted in the record are the highest and lowest for the year, hence we must estimate the price paid January 1, 1866, which we do by placing it half way between the high and low of the two years 1865 and 1866.

The value in 1885 is set half way between the high and low of 1885. His list, then, is as follows:

TEST No. 5, BOSTON—1866-1885

Par	Company	Price	No. Shs.	Amount Invested
$1,000	Amoskeag	$1,280	1	$1,280
1,000	Pacific Mills	1,890	1	1,890
1,000	Merrimack	1,220	1	1,220
100	N. Y. Cent. & Hudson River R. R.....	100	8	800
50	Reading	52	16	832
500	Boston Gas Light	770	1	770
100	Cambridge Gas Light	97	9	873
50	Metropolitan (Horse) Ry.	51	18	918
100	Cambridge (Horse) Ry.	95	9	855
100	Douglas Axe	115	5	575

Total investment $10,013

The annual return on his investment would have been as follows:

INCOME TEST No. 5, BOSTON—1866-1885

Year	Cash Income	Year	Cash Income
1866	$1,093.00	1876	$687.00
1867	1,106.00	1877	752.00
1868	976.80	1878	674.50
1869	1,018.30	1879	729.00
1870	925.00	1880	812.00
1871	970.00	1881	800.00
1872	1,085.00	1882	663.00
1873	966.00	1883	569.50
1874	891.50	1884	519.00
1875	761.25	1885	565.00

Total income from stocks (20 yrs.)........$16,563.85
* Income from $10,000 bonds (20 yrs.)...... 12,155.00

Excess income from stocks over bonds...... $4,408.85

Using the same basis as to rights, stock dividends, etc., which we have applied in previous tests, we find, after the greatest increase in the purchasing power of the

* See Appendix I for special study of a group of bonds for this period.

dollar that this country has ever experienced or is ever likely to experience, that his holdings in 1885 have a market value of $10,936, an actual increase, where, if no other factor than the appreciating dollar were in force, a drastic decrease was to have been expected.

It becomes increasingly evident that some other factor is at work in our common stock values, and before we are through we will set ourselves the task of discovering what this factor may be.

In this period the capital value of an investment in bonds would have shown a decided increase and the advantage of stocks over bonds is shown in a different form below:

	Bonds	Stock
Total income	$12,155.00	$16,563.85
Value 1885	12,395.00	10,936.00
	$24,550.00	$27,499.85
Original cost, 1866	10,030.00	10,013.00
Total gain	$14,520.00	$17,486.85
		14,520.00
Net advantage of stocks over bonds		$2,966.85

The basis and legend of Chart No. 4 are the same as in Charts Nos. 2 and 3, except that relative real values are shown in terms of the dollar of 1866. In this case, line AD, the upward movement in the value of bonds, exceeds the upward movement in line AC, the value of our stock holdings. The figures given under Test No. 5 show that the excess income from stocks more than offsets this gain in bonds without reinvestment. The line AE depicts the movement in the real value of our stock holdings plus reinvested surplus income, described under Supplementary Test No. 5, page 112.

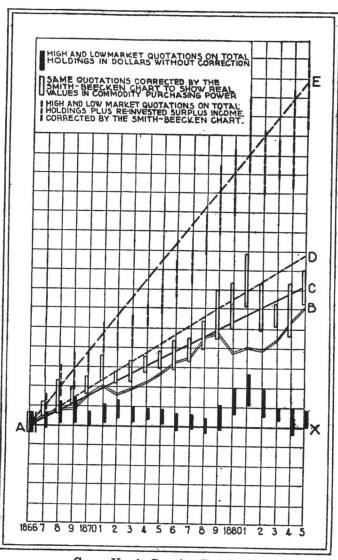

CHART No. 4—Covering Test No. 5

CHAPTER V

The results of Test No. 5, covering the period from 1866-1885, are by far the most significant. This was no ordinary period in the financial and industrial history of the country, but rather a period in which entered a variety of factors that would be expected to affect the earning power and ultimate value of common stocks adversely, while it favored long term bonds.

In view of the importance of this test it seems worth while to review some of the occurrences of this period:

STOCK PRICES

Babson's index of stock prices was not at as high a point in 1866 as it had been in January, 1864 (the peak), when it reached something over 140. It had fallen as low as 90 in 1865 but was up to 113 in January, 1866, falling to 92 in 1867, rising to 116 in 1869. From 1869 it went steadily downward until in 1877 it had reached 56. In 1881 it was up again to 122, then down to 78 in 1884, reaching 98 in 1885.

From 1885 to 1900 stocks showed no such violent major fluctuations as they did in the period from 1866 to 1885, yet we have seen how steady an income return was paid throughout the period on the diversified list of stocks selected for Test No. 5.

THE DOLLAR

Specie payment by the banks was suspended December 30, 1861.

Gold was quoted nominally at par January 1, 1862. In 1864, the price of gold ran up from 222 to 285 (July 1st) and back to 225 the same day. "Black Friday" occurred September 24, 1869, resulting from an effort to corner the gold supply.

Based on its purchasing power in commodities, the dollar was at its lowest ebb in 1864, gaining rapidly and almost continuously until 1878. Then it lost a little ground, but in 1885 was stronger than it had been at any time since 1864.

This movement of the dollar had had no counterpart since the Napoleonic Wars and has as yet had no other, though it is possible that the future may hold a similar movement in store for us, though if it does, the rapid increase since 1920 has taken the first edge off the movement. This recovery of the dollar since 1920 is very similar to its initial movement in 1864-1867, but has been much more rapid, having covered almost two-fifths of the ground lost since 1915.

Based upon the change in the purchasing power of the dollar there has never been a period which so favored the purchase of long term bonds as against the purchase of common stocks as the period from 1866-1885. We shall find, however, in our later pages that there is a force inherent in common stocks which is independent of fluctuations in dollar values, and accounts for the fact that in spite of the theoretical advantage of bonds over stocks in this period, the latter held their own.

COMMERCIAL PAPER

Average monthly high and low rates for commercial paper during this period were as follows:

Year	Low *	High *	
1866	5.45%	7.95%	
1867	7.00	10.00	
1868	6.40	10.15	During this period rates averaged well above 8%
1869	7.60	11.70	
1870	5.10	8.95	
1871	4.85	9.80	
1872	6.00	12.35	
1873	6.50	17.00	Panic
1874	5.45	7.40	
1875	4.30	6.65	
1876	3.60	6.45	
1877	4.00	7.25	
1878	3.60	5.85	
1879	3.80	6.25	During this period rates averaged well below 6%
1880	4.45	6.00	
1881	3.50	6.25	
1882	4.62	6.75	
1883	4.75	6.38	
1884	4.62	5.95	
1885	3.50	4.69	

Rates on commercial paper touched 8% again only for 2 months in the panic of 1893, 2 months in 1896 under threat of free coinage of silver, 1 month in panic of 1907 and 2 months in 1919. The low rates prevailing in 1924 should be noted.

There has never been since 1873, a period in which the purchase of long term interest-bearing bonds was more favorable to the investor from the point of view of yield on purchase price (unless perhaps a short period in 1920) than in the period from 1866 to 1873.

* Rates are taken from "Review of Economic Statistics," January, 1923—Harvard Economic Service.

PANIC OF 1873

This panic commenced with the failure of Jay Cook & Co., September 18, 1873, followed in rapid succession by the failure of other leading bankers and on September 20th, by that of two trust companies, three banking houses and the Bank of the Commonwealth.

The New York Stock Exchange closed its doors for 10 days, something previously unknown in its history, suspension of currency payments by New York banks, followed by banks throughout the country started September 22nd, and lasted for forty days. This was a suspension within a suspension as gold payments had been suspended since 1861.

That England felt this panic is shown by the raising of the Bank of England's interest rate from 3% to 9%.

The effects of the panic were severely felt by business interests through the long years following, and it was not until the fall of 1879 that the recovery was complete.*

NEAR PANIC OF 1884

The recovery was checked by the assassination of President Garfield in 1881, which was followed by reaction and liquidation until in 1884 six New York banks were in a failing condition and saved themselves only by pooling their interests.

It can be seen from the foregoing summary that our tests and comparisons of common stock and bond investments from 1866-1885 in no way favor common stocks while they do in marked degree favor long term bonds.

* Martin's "Boston Stock Market—88 Years." Other comments on this period are largely from the same source.

CHAPTER VI

ADDITIONAL COMPARISONS BETWEEN COMMON STOCKS AND BONDS

In view of the importance of this period in testing the position of common stocks, other tests seemed desirable.

In Test No. 6 the same general classifications of stocks are taken as in Test No. 5, except that the next largest companies are chosen, resulting in the following selection. There are two industrials and only one horse railway because two of the latter could not be found with complete tabulated records. This is without doubt unfavorable to our proposition because one of the industrials (Boston Sugar Refinery) ceased to pay dividends after the first seven years and had a total market value of $82 in 1885 against a total purchase price of $887 in 1866; and the other industrial, Boston and Roxbury Milling Corporation, was a most irregular payer.

It should be realized, moreover, that in going down the abbreviated list of the Boston Stock Exchange of 1866 until we were able to pick twenty stocks we were forced into a much smaller class of industry than we would be likely to reach if we selected several hundred stocks to-day.

The list comprising this test was as follows:

TEST No. 6, BOSTON—1866-1885

Par	Company	Price	No. Shs.	Amount Invested
$690	Lowell Cotton Mill	890	1	$890
100	Atlantic Cotton Mills	90	11	990
100	Bates Cotton Mill	160	6	960
100	Chi., Burl. & Quincy	119	9	1,071
100	Mich. Cent.	104	9	936
100	Chelsea Gas Light	93	11	1,023
100	South Boston Gas Light....	101	11	1,111
100	Middlesex (Horse)	58	18	1,044
1,000	Boston Sugar Refinery	887	1	887
no par	Boston & Roxbury Milling..	43	25	1,075

Total investment $9,987

The actual income from this group of stocks in comparison with the income from a group of the best bonds purchasable in 1866 was as follows:

INCOME TEST No. 6, BOSTON—1866-1885

Year	Cash Income	Year	Cash Income
1866	$908	1876	$407
1867	684	1877	409
1868	761	1878	529
1869	888	1879	425
1870	868	1880	539
1871	903	1881	1,136
1872	1,154	1882	540
1873	719	1883	472
1874	457	1884	457
1875	491	1885	422

Total income from stocks (20 yrs.)............ $13,169
* Income from $10,000 bonds (20 yrs.)........ 12,155

Excess income from stocks over bonds......... $1,014

Again the stocks win on income return, though in this case by a narrower margin and with greater irregularity of return.

* See Appendix I for special study of a group of bonds for this period.

The market value of this second group in 1885, contrary to what might have been expected, showed a slight gain as follows:

Original purchase price, 1866 .... $9,987
Estimated value, 1885 10,326

Taking into account the appreciation in capital value as well as the income return, our investor in bonds in 1866 would have had an advantage over our second list of stocks, but only to the extent of $1,012, as shown in the table following:

	Bonds	Stocks
Total income	$12,155	$13,169
Value, 1885	12,395	10,326
	$24,550	$23,495
Original cost, 1866	10,030	9,987
Total gain	$14,520	$13,508
	13,508	
Net advantage from bonds........ $1,012		

TEST No. 7—1892-1911

1866-1885 was, as we have said, the worst period for common stocks from the point of view of appreciating currency values. But there is another period which it seems desirable to cover, namely, 1892-1911. In 1892 stock prices were at a high point from which they descended rapidly in the panic of 1893. This panic was followed by what is considered one of the most severe industrial depressions accompanied by an unusually large number of failures and reorganizations.

We have, therefore, assumed the purchase of ten common stocks in January, 1892, selected upon the following basis:

(1) A group of railroad and industrial stocks of companies having the largest total capitalization in 1892 were selected.

(2) These were then grouped according to industries.

(3) One or two stocks were taken from each group on the basis of regularity of dividend payments over the period of from three to five years previous to 1892.

This resulted in the following list:

TEST No. 7—1892-1911

Common Stock	No. of Shares	Av. Price 1st Week 1892	Amount Invested
Chicago & Northwestern Ry.......	9	116	$1,044
N. Y. Central & Hudson River R. R.	9	116	1,044
Chicago, Burlington & Quincy R. R..	9	106	954
Western Union Telegraph	12	84	1,008
Consolidated Gas Co..............	10	104	1,040
Pullman Palace Car	5	185	925
Lehigh Coal & Navigation Co.	20	49	980
Adams Express Company	7	148	1,036
American Express Company	9	117	1,053
Edison Elec. Illuminating Co. (N. Y.)	12	80	960

Total investment $10,044

The increase in principal value of the stocks in Test No. 7 was as follows:

Original purchase price, January, 1892...........$10,044
Market value, December 31, 1911............... 17,419

INCOME TEST No. 7—1892-1911

Year	Cash Income	Year	Cash Income
1892	$661.75	1902	$687.60
1893	556.00	1903	711.60
1894	557.75	1904	896.60
1895	514.50	1905	737.60
1896	519.00	1906	852.50
1897	519.00	1907	780.60
1898	691.50	1908	756.20
1899	591.60	1909	799.60
1900	608.60	1910	1,013.35
1901	661.60	1911	831.85

Total income from stocks $13,948.80
* Income from bonds (yielding 4.80% in 1892) 9,600.00

Excess income from stocks over bonds ....$ 4,348.80

Again we find that ten stocks representing the largest companies in diversified industries have weathered two panics, and our war with Spain with income exceeding, in every year, the amount that could be obtained from an investment in high grade bonds. The capital value of the investment has increased 74% during the same period.

The total advantage of stocks over bonds in this test may be shown as follows:

Increase in market price of stocks, 1892-1911.. $7,375.00
Excess income from stocks over bonds 4,348.80

Total advantage of stocks over bonds $11,723.80

* Standard Daily Trade Service Bulletin No. 10, October 20, 1923.

TEST No. 8—1906-1922

In studying the high and low prices obtainable for our total holdings under the several tests described, it became apparent that if we had bought the securities chosen for Test No. 1, in January, 1906, they would have shown a capital loss between that date and December, 1922. In other words, those stocks which were chosen in 1901 were selling on the average higher in 1906 than they were in 1922.

We do not give much weight to Test No. 1, owing to the haphazard method by which the stocks were selected. But the fact that a group of stocks selected on any principle were selling higher in 1906 than in 1922, suggested that a test covering this period of 17 years might be desirable.

So we have made another study as shown in Test No. 8 and Test No. 8a. The reason for this secondary test is explained later.

THE LARGEST COMPANIES

Our aim in Test No. 8 is to select the largest companies in a diversified list of industries. We, therefore, first select the largest railroad from a stock issue point of view (the Pennsylvania). We then list the leading industrial companies in the order of the size of their outstanding common stock issues,* omitting only those companies which are obviously in the same industry as some company already listed.

This method of selection gives us the following companies as the basis for our test:

* Commercial and Financial Chronicle, Railway and Industrial Section, for January, 1906.

TEST No. 8—1906-1922

Common Stock Outstanding 1906	Common Stocks	Number of Shs.	Purchase Price	Amount Invested
$302,749,000	Pennsylvania R. R. (50).......	15	72	$1,080
508,302,500	U. S. Steel Corp.	25	43	1,075
153,888,000	Amalgamated Copper	10	110	1,100
131,551,400	American Tel. & Tel.	7	141	987
98,338,300	Standard Oil	1	697	697
80,000,000	Consol. Gas Co. (N. Y.)......	5	181	905
74,000,000	Pullman Co.	4	244	976
54,356,000	General Electric Co.	6	178	1,068
49,932,735	Internat. Mercantile Marine...	79	13	1,027
45,215,500	Corn Products	57	19	1,083

Total investment $9,998

The market value of these common stocks would have increased as follows:

Original purchase price, January, 1906........ $9,998.00
Market value, December 29, 1922 .... 14,135.25

Gain in principal $4,137.25

The yield on 15 high grade railroad bonds in December, 1922, was on a 4.88% basis, indicating that the holder of bonds over this period would have suffered an actual loss in the principal value of his investment unless all his bonds matured and were paid in full on the date selected for the valuation. Assuming, however, that he had no capital loss, his total gain by holding stocks instead of high grade bonds would have been:

Increase in market price of stocks, 1906-1922....$4,137.25
Excess income from stocks over bonds......... 2,513.76

Total advantage of stocks over bonds $6,651.01

The income return each year from these securities calculated on the same basis as in previous tests would have been in detail as follows:

INCOME TEST No. 8—1906-1922

Year	Cash Income	Year	Cash Income
1906	$498.53	1914	$466.19
1907	429.00	1915	401.39
1908	364.00	1916	559.94
1909	382.75	1917	787.96
1910	458.00	1918	796.86
1911	499.25	1919	509.46
1912	443.97	1920	709.26
1913	534.25	1921	656.46
		1922	680.53

Total income from stocks (17 yrs.)............$9,177.76
Income from bonds at 3.92% for (17 yrs.)*.... 6,664.00

Excess income from stocks over bonds $2,513.76

* Average yield of 15 high grade railroad bonds on prices at which they could have been purchased in January, 1906, as reported by Standard Statistics Service.

Test No. 8a

In Test No. 3 were included two stocks which were not paying dividends at the time of purchase. One of them, International Mercantile Marine, paid no dividends during the entire 17 years. The other, Corn Products Company, reorganized in 1906, the year of purchase, into Corn Products Refining Company, paid no dividends for 14 years from date of assumed purchase (1906).

It is entirely probable that no careful investor in 1906 would have included either of these in a purely investment list. Their inclusion in Test No. 8 serves to emphasize the power of diversification to offset unsound judgment in the selection of individual stocks or industries.

But in view of the fact that the holdings in Corn Products increased in capital value from $1,083 to $4,978, a net gain of $3,895, it seemed as if a supplementary test were desirable to make sure that this stock had not too greatly favored our leaning toward common stocks.

To test this we have excluded both International Mercantile Marine and Corn Products Co., on the general principle that no stocks should be bought that are not paying dividends at the time of purchase.*

We then examine the stock lists of the day and choose two companies, next in size of common stock issues, which are paying dividends.

This method brings into our list, in place of the two companies withdrawn, the following:

---

* This is not a sound assumption, to be sure, when complete analysis is possible.

Common Stock Outstanding 1906	Common Stocks	Number of Shs.	Purchase Price	Amount Invested
$45,000,000	American Sugar Refining....	7	154	$1,078
35,000,000	Swift & Company	10	104	1,040

Market value of stocks substituted.........$2,118

This is $8 more than the amount invested in the two stocks withdrawn from Test No. 8, making the amount invested in Test No. 8a, $10,006.

The income account in Test No. 8a shows a decided improvement over Test No. 8, but there is a much smaller increase in capital value, as shown below:

INCOME TEST No. 8a—1906-1922

Year	Cash Income	Year	Cash Income
1906	$626.53	1914	$585.19
1907	548.00	1915	522.89
1908	483.00	1916	1,022.27
1909	503.45	1917	1,081.96
1910	577.00	1918	1,019.36
1911	619.25	1919	675.46
1912	562.97	1920	747.26
1913	653.25	1921	561.21
		1922	548.53

Total income from stocks (17 years).........$11,337.58
Income from bonds at 3.92% (17 years)...... 6,664.00

Excess income from stocks over bonds........ $4,673.00

The increase in capital value was as follows:

Original purchase price, January, 1906........$10,006.00
Market value, December 29, 1922 .... 10,270.50

Gain in principal $264.50

The total advantage of stocks over bonds in this test would have been as follows:

Increase in market price of stocks, 1906-1922.... $264.50
Excess income from stocks over bonds.......... 4,673.58

Total advantage of stocks over bonds $4,938.08

CHAPTER VII

RAILROAD STOCKS, 1901-1922

There is a general impression that while rails were considered the prime common stock investment of the latter part of the nineteenth century, they have proved disappointing since 1900. In New York and Boston you cannot mention rails without hearing some one refer to the unfavorable experiences of investors in New York, New Haven & Hartford common stock.

This conception that railroads as a class have turned out to be less profitable investments than industrials, is so widely held that it has seemed worth while testing it with facts. Consequently we have made three tests of the results which would have followed the investment of three funds of $10,000 in the common stocks of railroad companies in January, 1901, holding the original investments until December, 1922. This is the same period covered by Tests Nos. 1, 2 and 3, which, however, include only industrial stocks.

We first selected the railroads which, in 1901, had the largest outstanding issues of common and preferred stocks. Living as we do, close to the seaboard, we were somewhat surprised to find that New York, New Haven & Hartford did not appear among the first twenty in this list.

From these, three groups of ten were selected upon which to base tests.

Test No. 9 covers the ten railroads with the largest stock issues.

Test No. 10 covers the ten railroads with the largest stock issues which paid dividends on their common stocks in 1900.

Test No. 11 covers the ten railroads with the largest stock issues which paid no dividends in 1900.

We do not intend to convey the impression by these last three tests that we would recommend an investment in rails to the exclusion of all other classes of stocks. But we offer them as definite proof that if we had included rails in Tests Nos. 1, 2 or 3, they would not have affected these tests adversely. Our data indicate that the three largest rails would have improved the results of these earlier tests.

TEST No. 9—1901-1922

This test covers the ten railroads which in 1901 had the largest amount of stock outstanding:

Common Stock	Number of Shares	Average Price Week of Jan. 12, 1901	Amount Invested
Atchison, Topeka & Ste. Fe...	20	48	$960
Southern Pacific	23	44	1,012
Union Pacific	12	82	984
Southern Railway	45	22	990
Erie R. R.	37	27	999
Northern Pacific *	12	85	1,020
Pennsylvania	13	75	975
Reading	80	13	1,040
New York Central & Hud. R..	7	145	1,015
Baltimore & Ohio	12	85	1,020

Total investment $10,015

Of these, neither Southern Railway nor Erie paid any dividends throughout the period, yet the annual income return from the above list was as follows:

INCOME TEST No. 9—1901-1922

Year	Cash Income	Year	Cash Income
1901	$288.00	1912	$848.00
1902	316.00	1913	928.00
1903	334.00	1914	1,023.85
1904	331.00	1915	911.00
1905	486.00	1916	911.00
1906	631.75	1917	953.00
1907	764.25	1918	897.50
1908	884.87	1919	920.00
1909	758.00	1920	860.00
1910	853.25	1921	850.25
1911	849.75	1922	832.25

Total income from stocks (22 yrs.)...........$16.431.72
Income from bonds at 4% (22 yrs.) †........ 8,800.00

Excess income from stocks over bonds $7,631.72

* This stock sold on the New York Stock Exchange, in 1901, as high as $700 per share. Private sales were reported at $1,000 per share. For the purposes of the test, however, it is left in the list. Its price, December 31, 1922, was $76 per share, showing a loss.
† See Tests Nos. 1, 2 and 3.

The market value of the holdings under this test at December 31, 1922, was $16,118, a gain of $6,103 over the purchase price in 1901. The total advantage of these railroad stocks over bonds for the same period may therefore be summarized as follows:

Increase in market value of stocks, 1901-1922....$6,103.00
Excess income from stocks over bonds 7,631.72
_____
Total advantage of stocks over bonds $13,734.72

Test No. 10—1901-1922

This covers ten railroads with the largest amount of preferred and common stock outstanding in 1901, which paid dividends on their common stock in 1900. They are listed in the order of their size on this basis:

Common Stock	Number of Shares	Average Price Week of Jan. 12, 1901	Amount Invested
Union Pacific	12	82	$984
Northern Pacific *	12	85	1,020
Pennsylvania	13	75	975
New York Central & Hud. R.	7	145	1,015
Baltimore & Ohio	12	85	1,020
Chi., Burlington & Quincy..	7	143	1,001
Great Northern	5	190	950
Canadian Pacific	11	92	1,012
Chi., Milwaukee & St. Paul..	7	148	1,036
Chi. & Northwestern	6	172	1,032

Total investment $10,045

The annual income return from the above list was as follows:

INCOME TEST No. 10—1901-1922

Year	Cash Income	Year	Cash Income
1901	$428.00	1912	$630.50
1902	466.00	1913	630.50
1903	489.50	1914	726.85
1904	492.00	1915	610.00
1905	507.00	1916	617.25
1906	565.25	1917	727.00
1907	664.25	1918	582.50
1908	750.87	1919	605.00
1909	614.00	1920	533.00
1910	638.25	1921	616.25
1911	646.25	1922	545.50

Total income from stocks (22 yrs.)...........$13,085.72
Income from bonds at 4% (22 yrs.) †........ 8,800.00

Excess income from stocks over bonds........ $4,285.72

* See note under Test No. 9.
† See Tests Nos. 1, 2 and 3.

The market value of the holdings under this test at December 31, 1922, was $9,089, a loss of $956 from the purchase price in 1901, yet taking excess income into consideration they showed a total advantage over bonds as follows:

Excess income from stocks over bonds $4,285.72
Loss in market value of stocks 956.00

Total advantage of stocks over bonds $3,329.72

Test No. 11—1901-1922

Having tested the ten largest rails which were paying dividends in 1900 it seems fitting, in the spirit of research, to test the ten largest which were not paying dividends in 1900.   On this basis we get the following list:

Common Stock	Number of Shares	Average Price Week of Jan. 12, 1901	Amount Invested
Atchison, Topeka & Ste. Fe..	20	48	$960
Southern Pacific	23	44	1,012
Southern Railway	45	22	990
Erie	37	27	999
Reading	80	13	1,040
Norfolk & Western	22	45	990
Colorado & Southern	134	7.50	1,005
Mo., Kas. & Tex.	63	16	1,008
Denver & Rio Grande *	30	33	990
Kansas City Southern	72	14	1,008

Total Investment $10,002

* Upon appointment of a receiver, January 25, 1918, we sold out this stock at the market ($4 per share) and assumed an income at 4% on proceeds as in similar cases in Test No. 2.

The annual income on this list was as follows:

INCOME TEST No. 11—1901-1922

Year	Cash Income	Year	Cash Income
1901	$114.00	1912	$764.00
1902	135.00	1913	710.00
1903	146.00	1914	710.00
1904	146.00	1915	710.00
1905	297.00	1916	748.50
1906	406.50	1917	756.00
1907	510.75	1918	736.80
1908	754.00	1919	736.80
1909	775.00	1920	736.80
1910	876.00	1921	1,138.80
1911	881.50	1922	1,160.80

Total income from stocks (22 yrs.) $13,950.25
Income from bonds at 4% (22 yrs.)*.......... 8,800.00

Excess income from stocks over bonds........ $5,150.25

The market value of the holdings under this test at December 31, 1922, was $21,992, an increase of $11,990 over the purchase price in 1901. The total advantage of the stocks over bonds was, therefore:

Increase in market price of stocks $11,990.00
Excess income from stocks over bonds 5,150.25

Total advantage of stocks over bonds $17,140.25

* See Tests Nos. 1, 2 and 3.

CHAPTER VIII

A NEW STOCK MARKET CHART, 1837-1923

These tests we have made are not in themselves conclusive, but cumulatively they tend to show that well diversified lists of common stocks selected on simple and broad principles of diversification respond to some underlying factor which gives them a margin of advantage over high grade bonds for long term investment. But in view of the speculative attributes known to exist in common stocks we are hardly justified in accepting stocks as an alternative to high grade bonds for long term investment unless we are able to isolate this underlying factor with a view to appraising its potency under varying conditions and the likelihood of its continued operation in the future.

It seems desirable, therefore, to make further studies of the data assembled in order to develop from them a picture of the results which would follow the holding of common stocks from the earliest date down to the present day.

MANY CHARTS ARE MISLEADING

The usual data and charts representing market fluctuations of common stocks are of no value in this connection, as they disregard stock dividends, the subdivision of shares, securities of different character given in exchange, and all the other changes in the form of holdings which would come to an actual investor in common stocks who retained the capital distributions on his original holdings throughout an indefinite period of time.

The gravity of the mistaken view which may result from the publication of such charts has been realized for some time by economists, but owing to the unpopularity of a more abstract presentation of stock market movements, it is only recently that the Standard Daily Trade Service has made the decision to change the basis of its stock market charts. The nature of these changes and the reasons for them are clearly set forth in their bulletin of October 25, 1923 (Vol. 30, page 219, and following). To explain the false picture that is presented by charts which give no consideration to stock dividends we quote from the above bulletin as follows:

Take, as an example, Standard Oil of New Jersey, which declared a 4 for 1 stock dividend late in 1922.

On July 1, 1922, this stock was selling at 181; on July 1, 1923, it was selling at 32. The percentage decline in *price* from one date to the other was 82.3%.

On July 1, 1922, the total market value of Standard Oil of New Jersey was $722,000,000; on July 1, 1923, $638,000,-000. The percentage of decline in *market value* was 11.6%.

This covers one class of error which creeps into the average stock market chart. The other results from the fact that a movement of ten points in the stock of a company with a total capitalization of $10,000,-000 will affect the curve of the customary chart just ten times as much as a contrary movement of one point in United States Steel. Yet a movement in Steel should be given just about fifty times as much weight as a movement in a stock of which only $10,000,000 is outstanding.

We are therefore forced to attempt to construct our own statistical series from the data we have at hand, and for this purpose have chosen the data underlying the following tests:

1866-1885, TEST No. 5

3 Cotton Mills.	2 Gas Light Companies.
2 Railroads.	2 Horse Railways.

1 Axe Company

1880-1899, TEST No. 4

3 Express Companies.	1 Railroad Equipment Company.
5 Railroads.	1 Telegraph Company.

1892-1911, TEST No. 7

3 Railroads.	1 Coal Co.
1 Telegraph Co.	2 Express Companies.
1 Gas & Electric Co.	1 Electric Light Co.

1901-1922, TEST No. 3

1 Express Co.	1 Traction Co.
1 Coal, Iron & Steel Co.	1 Gas & Electric Co.
I Railway Equipment Co.	1 Tobacco Co.
1 Steel Co.	1 Rubber Co.
1 Telegraph Co.	1 Sugar Co.

We have, then, data relating to four separate stock holdings covering various periods from 1866 to 1922. The data of no one group cover the entire period, but the several groups overlap and if we are able to discover that these differing groups of stock have the same investment rating in those years when they do overlap, then we shall be justified in the supposition that we have made no vital change in the investment character of our holdings if we shift them at their market prices from one group of stocks into another in those years.

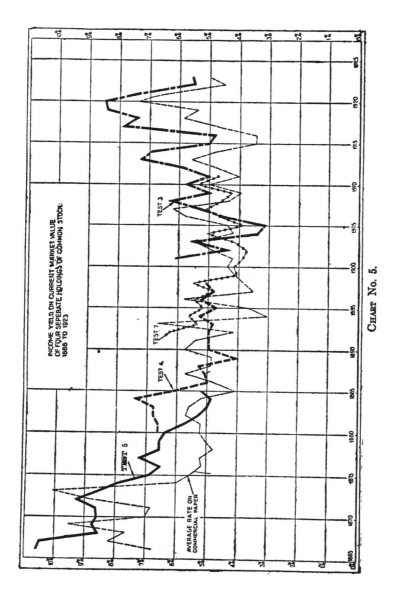

INCOME YIELD ON CURRENT MARKET VALUE
OF FOUR SEPERATE HOLDINGS OF COMMON STOCK:
1866 TO 1923

TEST 3

TEST 7

TEST 4

TEST 5

AVERAGE RATE ON
COMMERCIAL PAPER

CHART No. 5.

To discover if this is possible we have constructed Chart No. 5 upon which will be found:

1. The dividend yield on the yearly average market price of each group of stocks.

2. The yearly average rate on 60-90 day commercial paper.

A glance at this chart shows the measurably consistent relation that is maintained:

(a)   Between the yield on current market price of our holdings in the several groups in those periods in which they overlap.

(b)   Between the yield basis on all the holdings and the rate on commercial paper throughout the period covered by the Chart.   If for a time this relationship is not maintained, an adjustment follows.

We are further able to discover three points at which the stocks held in two overlapping groups may be considered to have the same investment rating indicated by the fact that the yield bases upon which two groups are selling are practically identical.   Such points occur in the years 1880, 1897 and 1906.

The consistent relationship shown in Chart No. 5 between the yields on the four groups of stocks we have used, each selected on a somewhat different principle, indicates, perhaps, that in preparing a composite series from data derived from these several groups we may be warranted in giving a wider application to our resulting conclusions than if the series were derived from a single group of stocks held throughout the entire period.

COMMON STOCKS, 1837-1923

Having established this consistent relationship between the market behavior of the several groups of stocks involved we may now proceed to the construction of Chart No. 6, which attempts to show the results that would have followed the investment of approximately $5,000 in 1837 in a diversified group of common stocks and held in common stocks until 1923, a period of 86 years. The method by which this is accomplished is described on the page facing the chart.

The picture here presented differs radically from any that we have seen relating to the market value from year to year of a fund invested in diversified common stocks, and tends to correct the erroneous impressions which are to be gained from the usual stock market chart. It also shows us in unmistakable terms why, in our tests, all of our holdings in diversified common stocks registered a gain in principal value at the end of twenty years. In fact, it becomes apparent that the longest period in which such an investment would be likely to have shown a loss in market value was for fifteen years following the peak of 1847. And even in this extreme case, as our chart shows only the average between high and low in each year, the chances are strongly in favor of our having had a number of opportunities during the intervening years to get out whole. Meanwhile it is evident, both from Chart No. 5 and from the data in all our tests, that our income would have been relatively stable during even such periods.

But we have yet to isolate the force which causes this continuous upward movement in the principal value of our stock holdings and to appraise the likelihood that it is still and is likely to continue operative.

CHART No. 6.

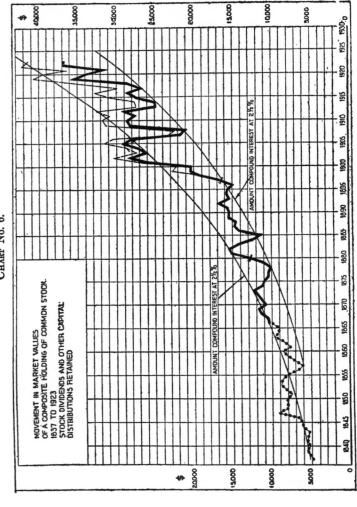

MOVEMENT IN MARKET VALUES
OF A COMPOSITE HOLDING OF COMMON STOCK.
1837 TO 1923
STOCK DIVIDENDS AND OTHER CAPITAL
DISTRIBUTIONS RETAINED

AMOUNT COMPOUND INTEREST AT 2½%

AMOUNT COMPOUND INTEREST AT 2½%

CONSTRUCTION OF CHART No. 6

With regard to this chart, we will first describe the solid line. This pictures a supposed investment in 1866 of $10,313 in the securities of our Test No. 5. The market value of these holdings, with stock dividends and other capital adjustments retained, is carried through 1880 when the holdings would have been worth $12,730. We then assume that these holdings are sold at the market and the proceeds reinvested at the market in stocks held under Test No. 4. These then are carried until 1897 when they are sold at the market and the proceeds reinvested in the securities of Test No. 3 held that year under Test No. 7. The final shift out of Test No. 7 into the securities of Test No. 3 is made in 1906.

It will be observed that these shifts have been made in those years when the holdings under the two tests involved are selling on approximately the same investment basis. (See Chart No. 5.)

So interesting was the picture presented by this solid line (1866-1923) that it seemed worth while to attempt to extend it further into the past.

For this purpose a group of seven stocks were selected concerning which records could be found covering the years 1837 to 1866 as follows:*

Stock	No. of Shares	Average Market Price 1837	Amount
Merrimack Cotton Mills	1	$1,180	$1,180
Boott Mills (Cotton)...............	1	1,000	1,000
Amoskeag Cotton Mills.............	2	955	1,910
Boston & Worcester R. R...........	15	87	1,305
Boston & Providence R. R..........	15	96	1,440
Boston & Lowell R. R..............	15	96	1,440
Boston & Roxbury Milling Co.	130	10¼	1,332
Total			$9,607

The average market value of this holding in 1866, including stock dividends received during the period, was $20,079. Dividing this figure by 2 gives us $10,039, which, considering the fact that we are dealing with yearly averages, is so close to $10,313, with which our solid line commences in 1866, that we have allowed it to stand rather than introduce a less obvious mathematical relationship which would not add to essential accuracy.

Thus, dividing the average market value each year of the above holdings by 2, we secure the spotted line from 1837 to 1866, which, with our solid line from 1866 to 1923, gives us a substantially accurate picture of the market value of the principal of an investment in common stocks made in 1837 and held in common stocks to 1923.

The light broken line from 1898 to date is described in the accompanying text.

*Martin's Boston Stock Market, 1798-1898.

CHAPTER IX

LAW OF INCREASING COMMON STOCK VALUES
AND INCOME RETURN

It is obvious that more than one force is at work on the market values portrayed in Chart No. 6, with effects that vary during different portions of the period, yet there seems to be some one force continuously at work.

The varying forces seem to find expression in the higher ranges, while the unvarying force appears to be expressed with some consistency in the relation of the successive low points in our chart.

For instance, viewing the higher ranges, we seem to have a series of steps. After a decided rise in values, the new high points established seem to define the high range for a period of from twelve to fifteen years, when the high range of that period becomes the low for the succeeding period. New highs are established by marked upward swings of from three to six years' duration. These steps are clearly defined in our solid line from 1866 to the end.

No emphasis is intended to be placed upon this series of steps, as the evidence at hand offers no basis upon which they can be explained, and there would seem to be no reason to look forward to their recurrence with regularity in the future.

THE FACTOR FAVORING COMMON STOCKS

But if we now turn to the low points, we cannot fail to notice the regularity of their upward progression which is continuous from the low of 1857 through the low points of 1878, 1885, 1896, 1908, 1914, to that of 1917, as shown in our solid line.

Joining these points produces a line which displays a gradually accelerating upward swing, a line that is strongly reminiscent of a graph representing the effect of compound interest at some constant rate.

That this resemblance has a basis in fact becomes apparent when after experimenting with other rates we apply a curve representing compound interest at 2½% commencing at the low point of 1857. The relationship between this line and our low points is too close to be without meaning, particularly as its implications are in strict accord with common knowledge of the practice aimed at by directors of conservatively managed corporations. Over a period of years these directors will never aim to declare all the company's net earnings in dividends. They will turn back a part of such earnings to surplus account, and invest this increasing surplus in productive operation. Such a policy successfully carried out is in fact a practical demonstration of the principle of compound interest.

A similar line representing compound interest at 2½% run from 1837 to date is not as satisfactory, but serves in a measure to help define the limits within which the market value of stock holdings may be expected to fluctuate.

Commencing in 1897, shortly after the major depreciation of the dollar set in, our holdings represented by the solid line begin to include bonds received as capital distributions, purchase money collateral trust securities, and cash distributions applicable to capital account. These tend to reduce the fluctuations of our solid line, and to dilute the purity of our common stock holdings. We have therefore added the light broken line which shows the movement in the market value of our holdings that would have followed the sale at the market of all bonds received and the reinvestment of the proceeds, together with any cash received in capital distribution, in the list of common stocks held, at the market for such stocks.

This seems to have raised the base of the low points in our heavy line, but on this new level they continue to display the same tendency and move upward at a rate which has been found to approximate 3.2% compounded, using the low points of 1908 and 1917 as bases.

Admitting the limitations of our studies, it would nevertheless appear that we had assembled sufficient supporting evidence to isolate the force inherent in well diversified holdings of common stock which has caused practically all of our previous tests to result favorably for common stocks as compared with high grade bonds over a long term—particularly as this evidence is in strict accord with the known aims of corporation directors.

We may even be justified, until contrary evidence is presented, in attempting to define the law controlling long term investment values as they are manifest in common stocks as follows:

*LAW OF INCREASING STOCK VALUES AND INCOME
RETURN*

*(1)   Over a period of years, the principal value of a well
diversified holding of the common stocks of representative
corporations, in essential industries, tends to increase in
accordance with the operation of compound interest.
(Chart No. 6.)*

*(2)   Such stock holdings may be relied upon over a term
of years to pay an average income return on such increasing values of something more than the average current rate
on commercial paper.   (Chart No. 5.)*

If we are ready to accept the law, not as proved, for
that is impossible, but as sufficiently indicated to warrant its acceptance as a measure of relative investment
values, then we have raised a standard for *long term*
investment which it will be hard to equal in any form
of maturing obligation—any bond, note, or real estate
mortgage.

Preferred stocks can be bought on a basis that will
compete with this standard only at infrequent intervals, and when they can, it is more than likely that
conditions are even more favorable to common stocks.

Bonds and preferred stocks which are convertible
into common stock upon terms that may be regarded
as reasonable under this law, offer a medium of investment that may be found, on analysis, to combine
both the protective qualities of bonds against short
term market fluctuations and the long term possibilities for capital enhancement which are present in
common stocks.

Having found that a well diversified investment in
common stocks, held over a long period, may be
counted on not only for a somewhat more than normal

income return (compared with current interest rates), but also for a definite increase in principal value, and that this increase in principal value is not based upon speculative factors but upon factors inherent in the nature of the security, we may formulate as a fundamental principle of sound investment that:

*In the selection of securities for investment, we must consider more than the expected income yield upon the amount invested, and may quite properly weigh the probability of principal enhancement over a term of years without departing from the most conservative viewpoint.**

* A somewhat similar conclusion is reached by Professor Arthur Stone Dewing by another approach.

CHAPTER X

We have found that there is a force at work in our common stock holdings which tends ever toward increasing their principal value in terms of dollars, a force resulting from the profitable reinvestment, by the companies involved, of their undistributed earnings. We have found that unless we have had the extreme misfortune to invest at the very peak of a noteworthy rise, those periods in which the average market value of our holdings remains less than the amount we paid for them are of comparatively short duration, and that even if we have bought at the very peak, there is definitely to be expected a period in which we may recover as many dollars as we have invested. Our hazard even in such extreme cases appears to be that of time alone.

In an attempt to measure the probability of this time element working against us, we have assumed the purchase of the holdings shown in Chart No. 6 at the average market price each year from 1837 to 1922, eliminating all bonds received from 1898 on, as described, and have asked ourselves for how many years immediately following the year of purchase these holdings would have shown a lower average market value than the price paid. There are 86 such years of assumed purchase (omitting 1923), and the result of our analysis of this time hazard may be summarized as follows:

			Cumulative Percentage
Number of times when the year succeeding the year of purchase shows no loss	54 times	63.0%	
Number of times when a loss in principal value lasts:			
1 year	13 times	15.1%	78.1%
2 years.........................	8 "	9.3%	87.4%
3 years.........................	2 "	2.3%	89.7%
4 years.........................	4 "	4.7%	94.4%
Number of times when a loss in principal value lasts:			
6 years.........................	2 times	2.3%	96.7%
7 years.........................	1 time	1.1%	97.8%
10 years.........................	1 "	1.1%	98.9%
15 years.........................	1 "	1.1%	100.0%

These figures, which imply the total absence of any judgment in the selection of the *time* when purchases are made, suggest that in buying a well diversified group of representative common stocks in essential industries, our chances of coming out even, or of making a profit in principal values, are: Within 1 year, 78 in 100; 2 years, 87 in 100; 4 years, 94 in 100.

There remain about six chances in one hundred that we should have to wait from six to fifteen years before having an opportunity to liquidate upon even terms. These are represented by five assumed purchases in the following years:

Year of Purchase	Number of Years of Lower Values, immediately succeeding year of purchase
1847	15 years
1853⎱ 1854⎰	10 " 7 "
1873	6 "
1882	6 "

The above dates are familiar to those who have made a study of conditions preceding major business depressions, and, in view of recent advances in economic theory as applied to investment problems, the reader may form his own opinion as to the likelihood of a well informed investor purchasing or retaining common stocks in these years. If he believes that the study of economics has been sufficiently advanced to forestall the purchase of common stocks at a time when a major boom in stock values has reached its climax, then he may feel confident that purchases made under sound economic guidance may be relied upon to maintain their principal values or to show a gain on an average as shown in the following summary.

By eliminating the peak years we reduce the number of years of assumed purchase by five to eighty-one:

		Cumulative Percentage
Number of times the year succeeding the year of purchase shows no loss	54 times or 66.7%	
Number of times when a loss in principal values lasts:		
1 year	13 times or 16.1%	82.8%
2 years......................	8 " or 9.9%	92.7%
3 years......................	2 " or 2.4%	95.1%
4 years......................	4 " or 4.9%	100.0%
	81 times or 100.0%	

In view of recent studies by Carl Snyder, which clearly show a continuous diminution of the swings of business activity above and below the line of normal growth, the fact that our time hazard in the purchase of a diversification of common stocks has not exceeded four years, since 1882, is significant.

CHAPTER XI

A FEW GENERALITIES

We have attempted to examine in a number of ways the results that would have followed holding diversified investments in common stocks during various periods, and have tried to measure the time hazards involved. Our results may seem to be more favorable than they have any right to be in view of the general practice of conservative investors, yet, viewing the situation broadly, it is obvious that this country could not hold the place it does to-day if a great majority of its industries had not prospered and had not produced the surplus earnings from which, in one form or another, capital becomes available for expansion.

That our corporations have so consistently been able to reinvest profitably a part of their surplus earnings may be attributed to the constant growth of population—or is it the growing population which makes the excess earnings possible? In either case it is interesting to observe that the rate at which the principal values in our stock holdings rose (Chart No. 6) is measurably close to the rate at which the population of the United States has increased since 1820, which averages 2.43% per annum.

Whether national growth is the cause or the result of successful industrial expansion may never be known, but the two work hand in hand in favor of equity values as represented by shares of stock.

The economists would say that it is the upward "Secular Trend" that favors common stocks as opposed to bonds, so long as the population and the business of the country are increasing. There is something more than growth of population that contributes to the rise in the "Secular Trend" and the increase in business from decade to decade. It is the constantly accelerating speed of modern life. All our activities are on a much more rapid basis to-day than they were twenty years ago, due in part to the constant increase in the speed of communication and transportation and the countless major and minor time-saving devices that have been introduced into our business and private life. All these have increased the annual turn-over per capita, increasing the rapidity of the circulation of money which is another form of depreciating what might be termed the social value of currency as opposed to its commodity purchasing value. All this acceleration favors carefully selected and diversified common stocks as opposed to bonds.

THE HUMAN FACTOR

There is another factor which favors a diversified list of common stocks in sound companies of good credit as opposed to bonds. It might be termed the "Human Factor" in the management of the companies involved. The management of every company is on the side of the common stock and opposed to the interests of the bondholders. The management does not want the bondholders to get more benefit from the operation of the company than is absolutely necessary to make it possible for the company to sell more bonds if such additional sale of bonds can be made to show a profit to the stockholders.

While in our tests covering the period from 1866 to 1885, we have given our bondholder the advantage of holding all his bonds to maturity, the records indicate that large parts of the issues involved and of many other issues purchasable in 1866 had been retired in one way or another before 1885. It was not possible to ascertain whether the actual bonds which our supposed purchaser acquired in 1866 could have remained in his possession until maturity or until 1885, but we do know that if there were any redemption clauses in any of the issues held or if there were any opportunities of buying the bonds on the market, the management of those companies whose credit was strong enough would have retired as large a part of those issues as possible and taken advantage of the decreasing interest rate to the disadvantage of the long term bondholder. If, then, our investor held any bonds which were called, or he weakened in his belief in the soundness of holding his bonds to the very end and accepted a moderate profit in principal by selling out at an earlier date, he would have lost a part of the total gain with which we have credited him in the tests.

DIFFICULT TO HOLD HIGH YIELD BONDS

In periods of high interest rates, such as were current in 1866, long term bonds are not freely offered, as the managements of issuing companies endeavor to protect themselves against the permanent payment of such rates. Anyone familiar with the bond market in recent years will recall the large amount of short term financing at high rates that was done and will also find that practically all of the bonds recently issued at attractive rates have a definite redemption clause which will be exercised by the management of the company, if and when interest rates show a definite and permanent decrease.

Thus, even in periods when underlying conditions favor the bondholder, there are factors at work which will deny him the full benefit which he had hoped for, while if the factor of a depreciating currency sets in, he will be called upon to suffer its full penalties.

We have before us to-day a case where the depreciation of currency has been carried by a highly organized commercial and industrial country, beyond the limit of anything previously imaginable.

GERMANY

What the final outcome will be in Germany cannot be foreseen, but we do know that the demoralization of currency values has completely wiped out the creditor class. The holders of bonds who depended entirely or in large part upon the interest that they received, became paupers. And the industrial leaders who, through the ownership of large blocks of common stock which control the processes of industry, and who were shrewd enough to use the depreciating Mark as a method of increasing their common stock control, are to-day the most powerful men in Germany. What the future holds for them at the hands of political powers outside of Germany cannot be foreseen, but to date, they have prospered inordinately.

Our own currency has depreciated very greatly in the last twenty years and our own holders of common stocks have profited in proportion, at the expense of our investors in bonds. We cannot foretell whether the dollar will appreciate rapidly during the next twenty years as it did in the period from 1866 to 1885, but our enormous gold reserves of to-day as opposed to our inadequate gold reserves of 1866 may lead us to question whether such a rapid appreciation is likely to occur.

STRONG FORCES AGAINST DEFLATION

All lenders of money, particularly bondholders, favor an appreciating currency. No other class is always actively in favor of an appreciating currency. In theory they all believe in sound or stable currency, but each, in his effort to widen the margin of profit that he makes in relation to profits in other lines, at times subscribes to activities which tend toward depreciation. Fortunately business men are both buyers and sellers. In buying they work for appreciating dollars, in selling they endeavor to depreciate the currency. Thus, with the bankers, who are both lenders and borrowers, their activities tend to effect a balance between the lenders on the one hand and labor, which always works for depreciation, on the other.

If our tests have been of any significance, they have shown that even in periods of appreciating currency such as the periods from 1865 to 1885 and 1880 to 1900, well diversified lists of common stocks in the largest and most important industries of the country have shown, on the whole, favorable results in comparison with bonds during the same periods. In periods where the dollar was depreciating, they have shown results so far superior to those obtained from high grade bonds, that there is really no comparison to be made between them.

There would, therefore, seem to be ample justification for including as a part of the investment of any large private fortune a relatively large proportion of sound, well diversified common stocks, selected not for their immediate market possibilities, but rather with their long term investment prospects in mind.

COMMON STOCKS TO-DAY

Fortunately for the investor to-day, in contrast to the supposed investor in our various tests, a wider and safer diversification is open in common stocks than at any previous date.

The growth of our industrial corporations both in number and size, since 1900, has been the most significant factor in the economic organization of the day. Prior to 1890 there were few corporations other than railroads, which had grown to the point where broad public participation was essential to permit their capital resources to keep pace with their opportunity for service. 1890 to 1900 was a period of experimentation in industrial consolidations and the development of corporate, financial and operating organization on the larger scale made necessary by the growth of the country and its consequently rapidly expanding demands upon its industries.

INCREASE IN NUMBER OF STOCKHOLDERS

To-day our railroads are estimated to have 807,000 stockholders. The American Telephone and Telegraph Company has over 300,000 shareholders, twice as many as in 1918. The United States Steel Corporation has almost 200,000, more than twice as many as in 1917, and General Motors, a comparatively new company, has 70,000 stockholders.

INCREASING RESPONSIBILITY

With increasing calls upon the public for financial support, has come increasing responsibility to so manage corporate affairs as to justify the continuation of this support. As the support of the public became constantly of greater importance both financially and for protection against unwise legislation the information available to the public concerning the financial condition of companies whose securities are offered on the public markets has also increased. A body of specialists in the analysis of corporate management and credit has come into being. These specialists in turn have gradually formulated what is fast becoming a science of corporate management, on the one hand, and of sound private investment in corporate securities on the other. The science, while still in its infancy, is recognized and is being developed in such institutions as the Harvard Graduate School of Business Administration, and in similar schools or departments in many other leading universities.

ECONOMICS, A GUIDE TO INVESTMENT

The study of Economics, up to recent years, has been treated as if it were purely a research and almost a philosophical subject, remotely related to the practical formulation of sound business and investment policies. To-day, on the other hand, it has its place at the council tables of practically all of the greatest business organizations, industrial, manufacturing and financial. The sum of these tendencies is constantly throwing additional safeguards around funds invested in the common stocks of our largest and best organized corporations.

That economic factors may in the last analysis prove to be those of the greatest importance to investors is suggested in the brief study of their effect upon bond values which are outlined in the following pages. No one may be regarded as having invested conservatively whose funds have suffered a permanent loss of real as opposed to nominal value. This is the first requisite of conservatism.

But it may be held as equally true that no fund is conservatively invested if it does not enhance in capital value at a normal rate approximating the average increase in equity values of the country as a whole, as expressed in dollars, after paying the investor a return commensurate with the rate obtainable on high grade bonds. We will look into the possibilities that this suggests a little later, but first let us examine some of the things that may happen to bonds; not such obvious things as failure to pay interest or principal when due, but some of the less obvious.

CHAPTER XII

FLUCTUATIONS IN BOND VALUES

In the various tests we have made of the relative long term investment values of common stocks and bonds we purposely avoided any emphasis upon the weaker aspects of an investment confined to bonds, in order that the results of our tests might not be subject to question. It is now desirable to draw another picture showing the real hazards in an investment confined to maturing obligations.

It is generally recognized that common stocks are subject to changes in market value, which may be at times rapid. But it is not so generally recognized that bonds and mortgages are subject to changes in real value almost as drastic as stocks, rarely as rapid, but perhaps more insidious in that they are not so easily appraised. The words "bond" and "mortgage" have for so long connoted security and safety, while the word "stock" has been so widely accepted as synonymous with risk and hazard, that an investor feels he is necessarily acting with more prudence and conservatism when he buys bonds and mortgages than when he buys stocks. Yet frequently this is not the case.

Let us, then, examine the underlying forces which affect the investment value of long term bonds. If we do this in connection with our studies of common stocks, we can hardly fail to see that we have still further grounds for the belief that, under proper diversification, common stocks deserve to have a far better long term investment rating than is usually accorded them.

BONDS 1902 TO 1920

A purchaser in April, 1902, of *Atchison, Topeka & Santa Fe General 4%* bonds, due 1995, or of *New York Central & Hudson River Railroad 3½%* bonds, due 1997, would have fared as follows if he had been forced to sell these bonds in July, 1920:

	Atchison 4s	Central 3½s
Purchase price April, 1902..............	103½	109
Basis (if held to maturity)	3.87%	3.20%
Same basis, July, 1920.................	103	108½
Market price, July, 1920	71	62
Loss	32 pts.	46½ pts.
Per cent of purchase price lost	31%	42.9%
Per cent of purchase price still held....	69%	57.1%

But the dollar in 1920 had only 37% of the purchasing power of the dollar of 1902, so that the real value remaining to the investor of what he actually invested in 1902 was as follows:

Atchison General 4s ....69 % x 37% = 25.53%
New York Central 3½s ....57.1% x 37% = 21.13%

In other words, he would have lost over 74% of the principal value of his investment in Atchison bonds; and over 78% of his investment in New York Central bonds, and none of this loss would have been due to any impairment in the credit position of these companies.

These illustrations, while extreme, focus attention on two elements of risk that exist even in the highest grade of bonds in addition to the element which is given most prominence by a majority of those who offer bonds for sale:

(1)   Depreciation of the Dollar.

(2)   A General Increase in Current Interest Rates

The third element which exists in some degree in all bonds and is most frequently discussed is:

(3)   The Changing Credit Position of the Debtor Company.

The credit position of a company is subject to change over a period of years, either through changes in management or policies, or through changes in the underlying price, wage, social, or industrial factors upon which prosperity of the company depends.

In the case of the two bonds cited, we have instances of heavy loss in principal value sustained by the holder of bonds of the highest character, due to an increase in the general interest rate and a coincident lowering of the purchasing power of the dollar.   There was no weakening of the credit position of the issuing companies.   These bonds have since recovered a part of their price loss due to a falling in the general interest rate since 1920, and have further regained a part of their lost principal value through an increase in the purchasing power of the dollar.   But it may be many years before a holder of these bonds purchased in 1902 will recover the full purchasing power of the funds originally invested.

There are bonds, moreover, which during the same period lost not only on account of the two causes first named, but in addition on account of the third cause: *A change for the worse in the credit position of the issuing company.*   Two such may be cited:

Chicago, Milwaukee & St. Paul Consolidated Mort-gage 4%, due 1989, bought in April, 1902, at 116, a basis to yield if held to maturity 3.4%. Such a price was justified only on the supposition that the bonds were entirely free from any risk of loss in principal value from any cause.

In the case of this bond all three of the hazards that pertain to bond investments came into play between the date of purchase and July, 1920, with the result that the bonds were quoted in that month at 60, a basis to yield 6.70%. This represented a loss as expressed in dollars as follows:

CHICAGO, MILWAUKEE & ST. PAUL CON. MTGE. 4%
DUE 1989

Purchase price, April, 1902	116
Basis (if held to maturity)	3.40%
Same basis, July, 1920	116
Market price, July, 1920	60
Loss	56 pts.
Per cent of purchase price lost	48.28%
Per cent of original investment still held	51.72%

But the purchasing power of the dollar in 1920 was only 37% of that for the dollar in 1902:

$$37\% \times 51.72\% = 19.14\%$$

Therefore, the actual purchasing power of the proceeds of the sale of this bond in 1920 would be less than 20% of the purchasing power of the original investment—a loss of over 80%.

Another example of the operation of all three factors against the integrity of an investment in bonds which were considered high grade at the time of purchase is found in the following bond of the New Haven System:

NEW YORK, NEW HAVEN & HARTFORD NON-CONV.
4% DEB., DUE 1947

Purchase price, April, 1902	117
Basis (if held to maturity)	3.28%
Same basis, July, 1920	113
Market price, July, 1920	46.50
Loss	66.50 pts.
Per cent of purchase price lost	58.85%
Per cent of purchase price still held	41.15%

37% x 41.15% = 15.23%

In purchasing power the principal value of the original investment declined in this case nearly 85%.

An improvement in the credit position of the issuing company obviously favors the principal value of an investment in its bonds. But the latter is only one of three main considerations and it may be interesting to show how it failed to offset the other two in the extreme period we have been considering. For this purpose we have selected a bond on the basis of facts which have become evident after the date of purchase, so that it cannot be supposed that an investor in 1902 could have made so fortunate a selection. The bond chosen is *Virginia Iron, Coal & Coke 5%, due 1949,* which sold in April, 1902, on a basis to yield 10% when high grade bonds were selling on a basis to yield less than 4%. The record in detail follows:

VIRGINIA IRON, COAL & COKE 5%, DUE 1949

Purchase price, April, 1902	50½
Yield (if held to maturity)	10.00%
Same basis, July, 1920	53
Market price, July, 1920	82
Gain	29 pts.
Per cent of purchase price gained	54.7%
Per cent of original investment held	154.7%

So far our investor would feel that his foresight in

1902, if it could be called such, had been rewarded by a handsome increase in the capital value of his investment. But if he then made inquiry as to what he could buy with the proceeds of the sale of his bond as compared with what the smaller number of dollars which he invested in 1902 would have bought at the time he invested them, he might not be quite so well pleased. The dollar in 1920 had only 37% of the purchasing power of the 1902 dollar:

$$37\% \times 154.7\% = 57.24\%$$

In spite of appearing to have made 54.7% gain in the real principal value of his investment he in fact lost almost 43% of it.*

In this instance a great improvement in the basis upon which the bond sold, which could be due only to an improvement in its credit position, overcame a general tendency toward higher interest rates, but was more than offset by a depreciating dollar.

It is recognized that thus to assign definite mathematical ratios to the fluctuations in the purchasing power of the dollar, is to enter a field in which controversy runs high as to which of various *methods* for measuring such fluctuations may be considered valid. In using figures derived from the U. S. Department of Labor, index numbers for Wholesale Commodity Prices, we have chosen the most convenient method available. All agree that the dollar fluctuates, and the results of these studies must be the same in principle, no matter

---

* It is quite true that this illustration has not been sufficiently analyzed to depict the exact situation, as the high rate of income return that he has received for the period has not been dealt with, but as it stands it serves to illustrate the point under discussion.

what method is used to compute its fluctuations. There is no intention in these pages of endorsing this particular *method* of estimating the practical effect of changing dollar values.

With this understanding, we may summarize the results of these illustrations as follows:

PERIOD COVERED—1902-1920

Three Factors Affecting Principal Value of Bond Investments

Bond	(1) Depreciation of Dollar	(2) Change in General Int. Rates	(3) Change in Credit Position of Company	Loss per cent in Principal Value
Atchison 4s, 1995	Unfavorable	Unfavorable	No change	74%
N. Y. Central 3½s, 1997	Unfavorable	Unfavorable	No change	78%
Chicago, Milwaukee & St. Paul 4s, 1989	Unfavorable	Unfavorable	Unfavorable	80%
N. Y., N. H. & Hartford 4s, 1947	Unfavorable	Unfavorable	Unfavorable	85%
Virginia Coal, Iron & Coke 5s, 1949	Unfavorable	Unfavorable	Very Favorable	43%

This summary shows in general terms what happened to investments in bonds made in 1902. And while most investors who bought bonds at or near that time are aware of a part of their losses, they do not all realize the underlying causes involved nor the force with which they operated against them up to the year 1920.

BONDS 1902-1913

The illustrations so far given have covered a period of extreme decline in bond values due to rising interest rates, as well as to depreciation in the purchasing power of the dollar, and so may be justly criticized as not representing an average, or even a typical period. The purpose in choosing this extreme period has been to show to what an extent the principal of an investment in bonds is subject to shrinkage. But in order to show that a great war is not necessary to produce similar losses, it may be well to see what happened to principal values invested in high grade bonds in 1902 if sold in December, 1913, before the war became a factor.

We again choose the Atchison and New York Central bonds of our first illustrations:

	Atchison 4s, 1995	N. Y. Central 3½s, 1997
Purchase price, April, 1902	103½	109
Basis (if held to maturity)	3.87%	3.20%
Same basis, December, 1913	103	108¾
Market price, July, 1913	95	81¾
Points lost	8	27¼
Per cent of purchase price lost	7.77%	25.06%
Per cent of purchase price still held ..	92.23%	74.94%

But the purchasing power of the 1913 dollar was only about 84% of the purchasing power of the 1902 dollar, hence the percentage of the real principal value of the original investment still held in 1913 was as follows:

Atchison .... (92.23% x 84%) 77.47%
N. Y. Central .... (74.94% x 84%) 62.95%

It appears, then, that if we regard the purchasing power of the money invested as the real measure of the investment, nearly 23% of such investment would have been lost in the Atchison bond, and more than 37% of it in the New York Central bond in a period that was not shaken by any world catastrophe (1902-1913) and yet the bonds had been purchased on a basis justified only by the supposition that their holders were free from any risk of loss in principal values.

Does this mean that bonds are not to be considered as sound investments at any time? Far from it. There have been periods when bondholders have profited greatly from favorable underlying conditions, periods during which the dollar increased in purchasing power while general interest rates were tending downward.

PROFITS IN BONDS 1866-1885

In connection with our Test No. 5 * a group of high grade bonds were assumed to have been bought in January, 1866, and sold in December, 1885. After yielding an average net income of 6.07% on the original investment, these bonds showed an increase in dollar market value of approximately 23.65%, so that the market value of the holdings in 1885 stood at 123.65% of the original investment. Meanwhile, the purchasing power of the dollar had increased to such an extent that the dollar of 1885 would buy 224% as much as that of 1866. An investor in these bonds then had during this period improved the real value of his principal (123.65% × 224%)—100%, or 177%.

The other group of bonds † which we studied were selling on a somewhat higher income basis in 1866, showing that they were not then regarded as of the best credit standing. These showed a gain in principal value by December, 1885, measured in dollars, amount-

* See Appendix I.
† See Appendix II.

ing to $3,000 on an original investment of $9,140, or approximately 32.8%. Thus the holdings stood in December, 1885, at 132.8% of the original investment after yielding an average annual income of 6.9% on that investment. Applying the increased purchasing power of the 1885 dollar, we find that the holdings in 1885 represented an improvement in position of (132.8% × 224%)—100%, or 197.4%.

Thus between 1866 and 1885 we have our bond-holders gaining both in dollar values, as a result of falling interest rates, and in the actual purchasing power of these dollars, while from 1902 to 1920 they lost heavily because of reverse tendencies in these two great underlying factors.

The percentages of loss and of gain to holders of bonds are larger than those which are customarily associated with bonds, and some who view the economist with a suspicious eye may say that the changing value of the dollar is a theoretical and not a practical loss or gain. It is well to ask these whether the loss in purchasing power of the Mark was a theoretical or a practical matter to the holders of German maturities payable in Marks, and to ask them further whether they believe that an income of $5,000 to-day is equal to an income of $5,000 in 1900 in the degree of social satisfaction it will afford.

In this connection the following item from the New York *Times* of June 7, 1924, furnishes food for thought. Exaggerated and fantastic as are all transactions in German Marks, they nevertheless serve to emphasize factors which are too often overlooked in their more moderate manifestations:

500,000,000,000% DIVIDEND DECLARED BY BERLIN'S RAILWAYS

The General Local Railway and Power Works Corporation of Berlin has declared a 500,000,000,000 per cent dividend on its common stock. Translated into terms of real money, the dividend represents $1.20 a share of 1,000 Marks value.

Previous to the war the same company paid a dividend of 10 per cent, which was then equivalent to $24 a share, according to figures obtained by the Foreign Department of Moody's Investors' Service.

Present holders of the 6 per cent preferred stock of the company, regarded as a high grade investment prior to the war, have been receiving 6 per cent per annum for the last year. This is equivalent to sixty trillionths of one gold mark. The entire issue of preferred stock recently was repurchased by the company.

It would seem that enough illustrations had been offered to dispel the idea that an investment in bonds was likely to remain of constant value, or that the selection of bonds of highest credit standing was any protection against the more important elements tending toward changing values which are to be found in the underlying economic conditions controlling the purchasing power of the dollar and the tendency toward higher or lower interest rates.

CHAPTER XIII

SUPPLEMENTARY TESTS OF COMMON STOCKS

REINVESTMENT OF SURPLUS INCOME

Going back to our original tests of the relative long term investment value of twelve separate groups of stocks and of high grade bonds, we discover that the favorable showing of common stocks in the comparison has been made even though one important item has been left out of the picture. We now want to bring this item into clear relief, as it is of the greatest importance to those who may be led by these studies to substitute a fair proportion of common stocks for bonds which they have been holding. It is an essential element in the sound investment management of a fund invested in common stocks.

Our lists of common stocks have, in every test, shown a higher total income than bonds for the same period. But in considering this surplus income, we have so far given no weight to the fact that it becomes available in small amounts annually and not in one lump sum, as we have shown it in the totals. Technically and actually, this has a most important bearing upon the relative merits of stocks and bonds as a medium of long term investment.

If we are to compare the results of long term investment in stocks as against bonds, it is not fair to stocks to assume that the excess income that they yield from year to year is immediately dissipated. This excess income over bonds, at a given time represents, in theory, the annual value of the additional risk involved in the purchase of a single stock as compared with the purchase of a single bond. We have seen that by diversifying our list of stocks, we have, in practice, eliminated this risk, while the public, by ignoring the fluctuating purchasing power of the dollar, has underestimated the risk attached to holding bonds.

REINVESTMENT OF SURPLUS INCOME FROM STOCKS

Let us, then, treat this annual excess income from stocks as a genuine reserve against the supposed risk of holding common stocks. Let us grant our investor the right to spend only the amount he would have received from an investment in bonds. Let us cause him to reinvest the annual surplus income from stocks each year as he receives it.

For convenience we will assume that such reinvestment takes the form of additional purchases of the stocks appearing in his original list.

The following supplementary tests show how such a policy carried out in connection with our original Tests Nos. 3, 4 and 5 would have affected the results of these tests. For ease of identification we give the supplementary tests the same numbers as the original tests to which they apply.

The stocks purchased in each succeeding year are taken in rough rotation from the ten stocks of the original tests. Deviations from strict rotation are necessary in order to employ as large a part as possible of the fund available at the end of the year, on the basis of stock quotations in January of the following year. Some stocks sell so high that not even one share can be bought, others at figures that leave too large an idle balance. In one case quotations were not available. Aside from these considerations the rotation of stocks is maintained.

We assume further that all dividends received from new stocks purchased are added to the amount available for investment in the following January.

The value of these supplementary tests is not merely theoretical. They point to an essential part of any investment policy which contemplates the purchase of common stocks. For while it is true that the income from the stocks in our various tests has rarely fallen, in a single year, below the income that could have been received from high grade bonds, yet above this point the fluctuations in annual return from stocks have been, at times, severe. There is danger that after a few years of high income, the investor might have so raised his standards of living that a subsequent dwindling of the income account would prove more of a hardship to him than if he had never received any of the higher income obtainable from stocks. Some plan of equalization is essential.

SUPPLEMENTARY TEST No. 3—1901-1922

ın Test No. 3, involving the purchase of ten stocks in January, 1901, to be held until December, 1922, the rate that could have been obtained on an investment in high grade bonds at the same date was 4% or $400 per year on $10,000.

During 1901 our investor received $616.60 from his stocks, leaving a surplus of $216.60 for the year, which we now assume he reinvested in January, 1902, in the first common stock appearing in his original list, but at the price quoted in January, 1902. Dividends paid to him on this stock in 1902 are then added to his excess income in 1902 to make up the amount available for investment in January, 1903, and so on. Carrying this out for the period of the test shows how the reinvestment of surplus income and its compounding, may increase the total of an investment fund:

ADDITIONAL RETURNS
SUPPLEMENTARY TEST No. 3—1901-1922

Year	Surplus Income from Original Investment	Dividends on New Stock Purchased	Total Invested Each Year
1901	$216.60	$......	$216.60
1902	115.00	8.00	123.00
1903	195.50	8.00	203.50
1904	6.00	19.00	13.00
1905	81.00	16.00	97.00
1906	332.00	44.00	376.00
1907	273.21	60.00	333.21
1908	363.85	62.30	426.15
1909	424.75	103.85	528.60
1910	562.75	154.35	717.10
1911	413.00	188.85	601.85
1912	585.15	245.85	831.00
1913	649.00	259.60	908.60
1914	608.75	347.30	956.05
1915	405.00	428.80	833.80
1916	409.00	486.05	895.05
1917	830.25	757.55	1,587.80
1918	768.50	875.80	1,644.30
1919	1,263.04	1,145.53	2,408.57
1920	1,240.54	1,274.36	2,514.90
1921	919.79	1,302.53	2,222.32
1922	714.04	1,345.45	2,059.49
	$11,364.72	$9,133.17	$20,497.89

It is apparent, then, that by reinvesting, each year as it came to him, the $11,364.72 which was the income received from stocks, over and above 4%, our investor has acquired an additional income amounting to $9,133.17, so that his total excess income over what he received on bonds has become $20,497,89 or more than 200% on his original investment.

But his new capital is in the form of stocks which have participated in the increases in value that a depreciating dollar and a speeding up of industry have caused. His holdings in December, 1922, in this reinvestment account were as follows:

Company	No. Shs.	Market Value Dec. 31, 1922	Amount
American Car and Foundry.......	46	160	$7,360.00
U. S. Rubber	23	56	1,188.00
Western Union Tele.	39	111	4,329.00
American Sugar Ref.	8	80	640.00
People's Gas Lt. and Coke	13	93	1,209.00
American Tobacco Co.	15	154	2,310.00
American Tobacco Co. B.	11	151	1,661.00
U. S. Steel	31	107	3,317.00
Bonds			
U. S. Steel 5s 1963 .... $237.00		104	246.00
Cash			
From U. S. Express sold out	160.00		
From B. R. T. sold out	437.00		
Available for investment 1923.... $2,130.00			
			———
			$2,728.00

Total value December 31, 1922.................$24,988.00

By adopting the policy of reinvestment that we have outlined, our investor in common stocks in 1901, would have received and spent the 4% on his original $10,000 investment and at December 31, 1922, his investment account would have stood as follows:

Market value December 31, 1922, holdings under Test
No. 3 .... $20,602.00
Market value December 31, 1922, on holdings resulting
from the reinvestment of surplus income. Supplementary Test No. 3 .... 24,988.00

Total value of holdings December 31, 1922 .... $45,590.00
    Original investment 10,012.00

Gain in capital value after deducting 4% per annum on
original investment $35,578.00

This is an increase in capital account of 355% in twenty-two years, or an average annual increment of over 16% on his original investment.

The conclusions to be derived from this test are too obvious for comment, and as we cannot count on the repetition of the underlying causes which brought this extraordinarily favorable result, we will pass quickly to other supplementary tests covering periods and conditions more nearly parallel to what we have a right to expect in the years immediately ahead of us.

SUPPLEMENTARY TEST No. 4—1880-1899

In Test No. 4 the investment in stocks in 1880 amounted to $10,163 and the basis upon which bonds were selling was 5.5%. This basis would give an annual income of $559 to the holder of a like amount of bonds.

Carrying this out for the period of the test, 1880 to 1899, gives the results following. These are not so dramatic, but they are very consistent, considering the period included one of the most pronounced depressions:

ADDITIONAL RETURNS

SUPPLEMENTARY TEST No. 4—1880-1899

Year	Surplus Income from Original Investment	Dividends on New Stock Purchased	Total Invested Each Year
1880	$180.00	$......	$180.00
1881	320.00	77.72	397.72
1882	365.00	36.00	401.00
1883	285.00	67.50	352.50
1884	241.00	89.00	330.00
1885	70.00	94.00	164.00
1886	63.00	88.00	151.00
1887	95.00	110.00	205.00
1888	115.00	129.00	244.00
1889	92.00	143.00	235.00
1890	113.00	158.50	271.50
1891	118.00	175.50	293.50
1892	175.00	213.83	388.83
1893	96.00	177.00	273.00
1894	165.00	228.50	393.50
1895	91.00	217.50	308.50
1896	128.00	243.50	371.50
1897	141.00	270.50	411.50
1898	326.00	325.56	651.56
1899	169.00	324.12	493.12
	$3,348.00	$3,168.73	$6,516.73

In this Supplementary Test No. 4 we assume that all income from stocks above $559 is reinvested as in Supplementary Test No. 3, and allowed to accumulate together with dividends on the new stock so acquired.

The surplus income over bonds of $3,348 has in this case brought an additional income of $3,168.73, raising the total excess income to $6,516.73, represented by the following holdings, which, by December 31, 1899, had so gained in market value that they would have brought a total of $9,208.11 as follows:

Company	No. Shs.	Market Value Dec. 31, 1899	Amount
Western Union Tel. Co.	8	85	$680.00
American Express Co.	8	146	1,168.00
Wells Fargo Express Co.	5	125	625.00
Chi. & Northwestern R. R.	6	159	954.00
Chi., Milwaukee & St. Paul	7	117	819.00
Pullman Palace Car	7	183	1,281.00
Del., Lackawanna & Western R. R...	9	88	792.00
Adams Express Co.	4	113	452.00
Bonds			
N. Y. Central 3½s 1997	$775.00	110½	1,961.38
Adams Express Co. 4s 1948	400.00	103	412.00
Cash			
Available for investment Jan., 1900...			63.73

Total value December 31, 1899 ....$9,208.11

After receiving and spending 5.5% on his original stock investment of $10,163, the investment account of our supposed purchaser of common stocks in 1880, would have stood on December 31, 1899, as follows:

Market value December 31, 1899, on holdings under Test
No. 4 .... $18,817.00
Market value December 31, 1899, on holdings resulting
from the reinvestment of surplus income. Supplementary Test No. 4 .... 9,208.11

Total value of holdings December 31, 1899 .... $28,025.11
Original investment 10,163.00

Gain in capital after deducting 5.5% per annum on
original investment $17,862.11

This represents an increase in capital account of 175% in twenty years, or an average annual increment of 8.7% on his original investment.

The bond basis of 5.5% is not far from the basis prevalent at the present time. The Standard Daily Trade Service shows the yield of 15 High Grade Public Utility Bonds for the first nine months of 1924 to have been 5.25% on their market price.

From 1880 to 1897 we have seen that the dollar continuously gained in value, falling off somewhat to 1899.

If we believe, then, that the dollar is to recover moderately in value from the present date forward, and if we believe that the great industries of the country are to continue the development which they have shown in the past twenty years, it would seem that a policy of reinvestment such as is suggested in Supplementary Test No. 4 might yield results approximately as favorable in the 20 years ahead as they did in the period covered by this test.

If, on the other hand, we hold with certain eminent economists, that there are no factors at present in sight that indicate any decided reduction in commodity prices during the next ten years—in other words, that the dollar cannot be counted on for any immediate further appreciation—then we should be led to expect a somewhat more favorable result from the adoption of such a reinvestment policy, than that indicated in this test.

Supplementary Test No. 5—1866-1885

The bonds in Test No. 5 yielded an average return over the entire period of the test of 6.07%,* but our investor in 1866 could not have foreseen this. So in this Supplementary Test No. 5 we allow him to deduct $660 annually from the income he receives from his stocks. This is the amount of income he would have received in 1866 from his bonds, and is approximately $53 more per year than the bonds yielded him during the whole term of the test.

*See Appendix I.

On this basis, which is distinctly in favor of the bonds, the results from a policy of reinvestment would have been as follows:

SUPPLEMENTARY TEST No. 5—1866-1885
ADDITIONAL RETURNS

Year	Surplus Income from Original Investment	Dividends on New Stock Purchased	Total Invested Each Year
1866	$433.00	$......	$433.00
1867	466.00	24.00	490.00
1868	316.80	68.00	384.80
1869	358.30	102.00	460.30
1870	265.00	146.00	411.00
1871	310.00	170.00	480.00
1872	425.00	214.00	639.00
1873	306.00	255.00	561.00
1874	231.50	259.50	491.00
1875	101.25	316.50	417.75
1876	27.00	330.00	357.00
1877	92.00	371.00	463.00
1878	14.50	381.50	396.00
1879	69.00	366.00	435.00
1880	152.00	467.00	619.00
1881	140.00	494.00	634.00
1882	3.00	526.00	529.00
1883	− 90.50	552.00	461.50
1884	− 141.00	493.00	352.00
1885	− 95.00	495.50	400.50
	$3,363.85	$6,031.00	$9,394.85

We find in this case that his surplus income of $3,363.85 has brought an additional income of $6,031, bringing his total excess income over bonds up to $9,394.85, represented by the following holdings, which in December, 1885, had an approximate market value as indicated:

Company	No. Shs.	Approximate Market Value December, 1885	Amount
N. Y. Central R. R.	17	94.50	$1,606.50
Metropol. Horse Ry. (Boston)..	34	91.50	3,111.00
Cambridge Gas	10	150.00	1,500.00
Douglas Axe	18	84.00	1,512.00
Cambridge Horse Ry.	16	83.00	1,328.00
Cash available for investment 1886			425.85

Total value, December, 1885 ....$9,483.35

After receiving and spending 6.60% on his original investment of $10,013 the investment account of our supposed purchaser of common stocks, in 1866, would have stood in December, 1885, approximately as follows:

Market value December, 1885, on holdings under Test
No. 5 .... $10,936.00
Market value December, 1885, on holdings resulting from
the reinvestment of surplus income. Supplementary
Test No. 5 .... 9,483.35

Total value of holdings December, 1885 .... $20,419.35
Original investment 10,013.00

Gains in capital after deducting 6.60% per annum on
original investment $10,406.35

This represents an increase in capital account of 104% in twenty years, or an average annual increment of 5.2% on his original investment.

It is this test, giving as it does every advantage to bonds, in a period which more than any other period favored bonds, that we believe indicates conclusively the merits of an investment in well diversified common stocks accompanied by a policy of reinvested surplus income.

CHAPTER XIV

INVESTMENT MANAGEMENT

The three supplementary tests that we have just outlined are particularly significant as they suggest one step toward investment management. To take this step involves action on the part of the investor. He must keep adequate records and exercise judgment from time to time in wisely reinvesting his surplus income.

In buying bonds, an investor reduces his own routine to a minimum. He accepts the stipulated rate of income provided by the terms of the bond and delegates to the issuing companies all responsibility for setting aside adequate reserves to protect this stipulated income, and he delegates to them the exercise of judgment in reinvesting these reserves. In fact, he delegates to them the entire management of his invested funds.

To compensate them for this management, for relieving him of all responsibility and of keeping all but the simplest of records, the investor agrees that the issuing companies may retain all earnings over and above the income return which he has agreed to accept. He establishes no reserves of his own, and relinquishes all title to the reserves that are established for him. Such reserves, while protecting his income, accrue to the benefit of the stockholders of the companies whose bonds he holds.

The purchaser of a bond is an investor, but he exercises none of the functions of investment management with regard to his invested funds. He pays the corporation which issues the bonds a substantial sum for exercising this function for him, and a survey of the prices at which bonds in different industries sell discloses the fact that he pays on the average more for this service in those industries whose stabilized earnings call for the least responsibility on the part of the issuing companies.

This illustrates the distinction which is to be drawn between the meaning of the terms "Investment" and "Investment Management." "Investment" implies a single act, and implies the exercise of sound judgment only at the time the investment is made. "Investment Management" is a continuing act and implies the continuous application of judgment. It includes the act of investment, but it also includes a great deal more.

A fund invested at a given time is entitled to a certain return under the conditions prevailing or to be foreseen at that time. A fund placed under competent investment management is entitled to this same return plus an additional return which is large or small in proportion to the degree of investment management that may be applied to it, and the ability of those who apply it.

Our supplementary tests have shown only one of the functions of investment management, and not the most important of them.

Investment Management includes the function of

establishing a just relation between that portion of income which may be safely spent, and that part which should be reinvested for the protection of this income and the enhancement of the fund, but its principal opportunity lies in appraising current economic and industrial conditions as they tend to affect the holdings of the fund.

In our section devoted to bonds we have seen how unimportant a splendid credit position proved to be in comparison with the more fundamental factors relating to the tendency in interest rates and the purchasing power of currency over a long period of years. But we have not touched upon the opportunities open to investment management at different stages of shorter economic cycles, through shifting from common stocks representing equities into maturing obligations and thereafter returning to common stocks. Such opportunities have existed in the past and have been in many instances defined with sufficient clarity to be used to the material advantage of funds under informed investment management.

Sound investment management takes these economic factors into consideration in determining at any given time what proportion of a fund should be in equities represented by common stocks and what proportion should be in maturing obligations represented by bonds, and is vigilant to note changes in fundamental conditions which dictate a change in these proportions. But investment management goes further.

In our various tests, the industries and the specific stocks were chosen with a minimum of judgment. This insured the value of the tests from the point of view of pure research. But in actual practice sound investment management based on wide knowledge of current industrial conditions and of the character of management existing in various companies within the most promising industries would certainly have improved the selection both as to industries and as to specific securities.

Sound investment management, while always subject to error, cannot fail to improve average investment results if the principal of diversification is strictly adhered to.

But diversification may be carried to excess. No investor nor group of men responsible for any investment fund can keep constantly informed regarding too long a list of securities representing too wide a variety of industries, locations and managements. There are well recognized limitations to the diversity of items upon which continuous judgment may be exercised. Better results are obtained when these limitations are admitted as facts.

We may, then, summarize the principal functions of Investment Management as follows:

1. It will first establish a sound investment plan suitable to the purposes of the investor.

2. It will then determine what proportion of the fund under its management shall be in equities and what proportion in bonds under current industrial and economic conditions.

3. It will put itself in a position to watch for changes in conditions and be prepared to modify these proportions in harmony with such changes.

4. It will study the current conditions of various industries and groups of industries, and will select as its field a

diversification of those which upon reliable data may be regarded as the more promising.

5. It will then examine the management and financial structure of the leading companies in these industries.

6. It will watch for changes both in the conditions of industries and of individual corporations and be prepared to change the investment to accord with sound analysis of the latest available information.

7. It will retain diversification as its fundamental principle, but will establish reasonable limitations to diversification in order not to dilute the quality of management applied.

This is no simple task. It is a task which each individual investor, responsible not only for his own welfare but for the welfare of those he is to leave behind him, must appraise in relation both to his own experience and training in a highly technical field and in relation to the amount of time and the facilities at his disposal to properly undertake it.

The writer believes that it is a task that can be properly undertaken only by an organization in which men of varied experience and training in the financial field unite with the single purpose of applying their best combined judgment continuously, with the least managerial complications, to the supervision of a single investment fund in which a large number of individual investors may participate. Thus, alone, may the best results be obtained.

APPENDIX

APPENDIX I

RETURN FROM BONDS, 1866-1885

As our whole study has been to compare the long term investment results to be obtained by the purchase of a well diversified list of common stocks with the results from a list of the most conservative bonds, we chose for our bonds those first mortgage railroad bonds which, in 1866, were selling on the lowest yield basis, thus showing that they were the most highly esteemed from a credit point of view at that time. The figures for bonds in Tests Nos. 5 and 6 are from the following list of bonds so selected. All are first mortgage bonds: *

Road	Rate	Maturity	(Notes)	Purchase Price, 1886
Pennsylvania Railroad	6%	1880	(6)	$1,020
Baltimore & Ohio R. R.	6	1885	(8)	1,000
Illinois Central Railroad	7	1875	(4)	1,060
Philadelphia & Erie Railroad	6	1881	(7)	970
Hudson River Railroad	7	1870	(1)	1,020
Chicago, Rock Island Railroad	7	1870	(2)	1,020
Del., Lack. & Western Railroad	7	1875	(5)	1,020
N. Y. Central R. R.	6	1883	(9)	920
Pitts., Ft. Wayne & Chi. Railroad	7	1912		1,000
N. Y. & Harlem Railroad	7	1873	(3)	1,000
				$10,030

* This was a period of high coupon rates, and the fact that bonds paid 6% and 7% in no way implied a lack of sound credit, or ample security. These were the standard high grade investment bonds of the day.

121

NOTE—As bonds matured and were paid, a new investment was made as follows:

	Date Paid	Amt. Rec'd	Reinvested in	Price
(1)	1870	$1,000	Central Pac. 1st 6s (1895)	$950
(2)	1870	1,000	Central Pac. 1st 6s (1895)	930
(3)	1873	1,000	St. L. & Iron Mt. 1st 7s (1892)	985
(4)	1875	1,000	Morris & Essex 1st 7s (1914)	1,140
(5)	1875	1,000	N. Y. Cent. & H. R. R. R. 1st 7s (1903)..	1,110
(6)	1880	1,000	C. R. I. & Pac. 6s (1917)	1,250
(7)	1881	1,000	Lehigh Valley 1st 6s (1898)	1,340
		$7,000		**$7,705**

Thus, $705, excess cost of new bonds, has to be deducted from income.

(8) Extended to 1935 at 4%
(9) Extended to 1893 at 5%

INCOME FROM BONDS

The total interest received on the above bonds was $12,860, from which deduct $705, leaving net income from bonds $12,155, as used in Tests Nos. 5 and 6.

The market value of the revised holdings in 1885 was $12,395, against original cost of $10,030, a gain of $2,365.

Income (disregarding $705 deduction) was as follows:

1866-69 inclusive	$660 each year	
1870	645	
1871-82 inclusive	640 each year	Average after deducting $705 reinvested 6.07%
1883	635	
1884-85	630 each year	

APPENDIX II

RETURN FROM BONDS, 1866-1885

(SECOND GROUP)

Fearing that some might charge us with unduly favoring common stocks by selecting bonds that were selling in 1866 on the *lowest* yield basis, although we know of no better way of appraising current opinion as to safety of principal, we selected a second list of first mortgage railway bonds purchasable in 1866, basing our choice on largest issues with the longest maturities showing a high yield on the purchase price. One of the bonds so chosen was overtaken by some sort of embarrassment, the outcome of which could not be traced, so it was stricken from the list and another inserted.

Thus, everything was in favor of this second list, as follows:

			(Notes)	Purchase Price, 1866
Pittsburgh, Ft. Wayne & Chi. Ist...	7%	1912		$1,000
Mich. So. & No. Indiana 1st	7	1885	(3)	940
Milwaukee & St. Paul 1st.........	7	1893		800
Marietta & Cincinnati 1st.........	7	1892	(4)	860
Baltimore & Ohio 1st.............	6	1885	(5)	1,000
Chicago & Alton 1st.............	7	1893		930
St. L., Alton & Terre Haute 1st....	7	1894		870
Chicago & Milwaukee 1st	7	1898		850
N. Y. Central 1st	6	1883	(1)	920
Philadelphia & Erie 1st...........	6	1881	(2)	970

$9,140

NOTES

(1) Extended to 1893 at 5%.

(2) Paid 1881, reinvested in Lehigh Valley 1st 6% (1898), $1,340.

(3) Paid 1885, reinvested in Lake Shore & Michigan Southern 1st 7s (1900), $1,290.

(4) Company in receivership June, 1877—sold bond at $1,010, reinvested in Erie Railway 1st 7s (1897) at $1,130.

(5) Extended to 1935 at 4%.

Reinvestment called for a deduction of $750 from total income.

Income ran at $670 per year from 1866 to 1882, inclusive, $665 in 1883, $660 in 1884 and 1885.

```
Total income  ...........$13,375 for 20 years
Less excess investment....    750
                          _____
Net income  .............$12,625 for 20 years
Average  .................    631
Or.......................6.9% on an investment of  $9,140
The value of bonds held in 1885 was..............$12,140
Original purchase price ..........................  9,140
                                                  _____
Gain in value of principal .......................  $3,000
```

This is probably the most favorable bond investment that could have been made in 1866 by a man who foresaw the value of long term holdings. They represent a list of bonds which benefitted in market price not alone as a result of a general fall in interest rates from those prevailing in 1866 to the lower rates of 1885, but also as a result of an improvement in the credit rating of the bonds themselves. They not only moved upward with the whole list of bonds, but rose to a higher relative position within the field of bond values.

Applying the figures of this second list of bonds to our Tests Nos. 5 and 6 in place of the more conservative bonds heretofore shown gives the following:

TEST No. 5—SECOND LIST OF BONDS

	Bonds	Stocks
Total income	$12,625	$16,563.85
Value 1885	12,140	10,936.00
	$24,765	$27,499.85
Original cost, 1866	9,140	10,013.00
Net gain	$15,625	$17,486.85
Net gain from stocks over bonds........		$1,861.85

TEST No. 6—SECOND LIST OF BONDS

	Bonds	Stocks
Total income	$12,625	$13,169.00
Value 1885	12,140	10,326.00
	$24,765	$23,495.00
Original cost	9,140	9,987.00
Net gain	$15,625	$13,508.00
	13,508	
Net gain, bonds over stocks....	$2,117	

APPENDIX III

RETURN FROM BONDS, 1880-1899

In Tests Nos. 1, 2 and 3 the assumption has been that the investor got his full income return for the full period at the rate indicated by the basis upon which high grade bonds were quoted in January, 1901, namely, 3.95%, and that he suffered none of the loss in principal which is implied by the fact that high grade bonds were selling in December, 1922, on a 4.88% basis. Those who are familiar with the principles upon which the yield basis of a bond is calculated will recognize the impossibility of calculating what this loss in principal would be, without establishing a set of hypothetical maturities for the bonds. We, therefore, give the bonds the benefit of all doubts and assume that they lost nothing in principal value, a thing that could have happened only if all the bonds matured and had been paid in full on January 1, 1923.

In the case of Test No. 4, however, we cannot assume that the investor in high grade bonds would not have benefited by an appreciation in his capital account, for while such bonds were selling in January, 1880, on a basis to yield approximately 5.5%, they sold in January, 1900, on a basis to yield 4.11%, implying a definite appreciation in principal.

It seems desirable, therefore, to check the yield and

any changes that might occur in capital value of a fund invested in ten bonds bought in January, 1880, and held till December, 1899.

The bonds chosen are the ones that existed in 1880 in a similar test covering the period 1866 to 1885, described in Appendix I in connection with Tests Nos. 5 and 6. These bonds, hypothetically purchased in January, 1880, were as follows—they are all first mortgage railroad bonds.

BOND LIST—1880

Road	Rate	Maturity	Notes		Purchase Price, 1880
1 Baltimore & Ohio	6%	1885	(4)	(10)	$1,080
1 Morris & Essex	7	1914			1,260
1 Pennsylvania	6	1880	(1)		1,020
1 Philadelphia & Erie	6	1881	(2)	(9)	1,030
2 Central Pacific	6	1895-9	(8)		2,164
1 N. Y. Cent. & Hud. River	7	1903			1,230
1 N. Y. Central	6	1883	(3)	(5)	1,045
1 Pitts., Ft. Wayne & Ohio.	7	1912			1,240
1 St. Louis & Iron Mountain	7	1892	(6)	(7)	1,150

Total investment $11,219

In 1880 the income on this investment was $650, or 5.8% on the amount invested, as against the 5.5% basis given in Test No. 4. But let us follow the history of these bonds, making reasonable substitutions when they are paid, but continuing to hold them when they are extended.

Note—The numbers before each of the following paragraphs refer back to the numbers in parentheses in the preceding list of bonds.

(1) In 1880 these bonds were paid off and the proceeds reinvested in 1 Chicago, Rock Island and Pacific 1st 6%, due 1917, costing $1,250, calling for an additional investment of $250.

(2)   In 1880 these bonds were paid and proceeds reinvested in 1 Lehigh Valley 1st 6%, due 1898, costing $1,340 and calling for an additional investment of $340.

(3)   In 1883 this bond was extended to 1893 at 5%, affecting one coupon in 1883.

(4)   In 1885 this bond was extended to 1935 at 4%, affecting 1886 coupons.

(5)   In 1893 the bond referred to in Note (3) above, was extended to 1905 at 4%, affecting one coupon in 1893.

(6)   In 1892 this bond was extended to 1897 at 5%, affecting no coupons in 1892.

(7)   In 1897 the bond referred to in Note (6) above, was again extended to 1947 at 4½%, affecting one coupon in 1897. In 1899 the issue so created was retired and the proceeds reinvested in B. & O. 3½%, due 1925 at 96.

(8)   In 1899, company reorganized, receives for each bond held: $1,000, 4% bonds due 1949; $50, 3½% bonds, due 1929; $29.17 cash (interest from February to August 1, 1899).

(9)   In 1898 this bond was extended to 1948 at 4%, affecting one coupon in 1898.

(10) Company reorganized.   Received in exchange: $1,025, 3½% bonds, due 1925; $125, 4% bonds, due 1948; $140, preferred stock; $10 cash (interest from April 1 to July 1, 1898).

The above will indicate how it came about that the income from an investment in bonds which yielded 5.80% on the amount invested, failed to maintain this rate throughout.

The investment December 31, 1880, amounted to $11,219; it increased in 1881 to $11,809; in 1898 it decreased to $11,609.

It was impossible to keep the whole fund continuously invested in these bonds. The percentage of income return on the amount invested in each year started at 5.8% but gradually declined until in 1899 it amounted to 4.75%. The average return on the average amount invested throughout the period was 5.17%, as against 5.5% allowed in Test No. 4.

The market value of the original bonds held in 1880 was..... $11,219
Additional investment called for 590

Maximum investment $11,809

The market value of bonds held December, 1899, was....... $11,536
Cash recovered through reinvestments 200

Total value of holdings, December, 1899 .... $11,736
Loss in capital value of bonds $73

Therefore, we are in no way favoring stocks when in Test No. 4 we assume that 5.5% was received on the bonds throughout the period of this test with neither gain nor loss in the principal invested.

Lightning Source UK Ltd.
Milton Keynes UK
UKHW041535270220
359443UK00001B/343